The Herbal Yearbook

Written and compiled by Gillian Haslam

Designed by Paul Turner and Sue Pressley

Photography by Paul Turner and Sue Pressley

Recipe photographs by Colour Library Books Ltd

Typesetting by DSP

Illustrations by Elaine Hill

Craft items made by Marion Haslam

Director of Production: Gerald Hughes

Production: Ruth Arthur; Sally Connolly

CLB 3231

Colour separations by Scantrans PTE Ltd, Singapore
Printed and bound in Spain
ISBN 0-85833-010-6

Additional Photography

The Garden Picture Library
Clive Boursnell: *June intro*, *Oct 22*, *Dec 15*; Linda Burgess: *page 9*, *March intro*, *Mar 22*, *July intro*, *Nov 8*; Brian Carter: *June 22*, *June 29*, *Aug 8*; John Glover: *Aug 1*; Mayer/Le Scanff: *Aug 29*; Jerry Pavia: *Oct 22*, *Dec intro*; Stephen Robson: *Nov 15*; David Russell: *Jan 22*, *Nov 22*, *Nov 29*, *Dec 1*, *Dec 8*; Brigitte Thomas: *Oct 8*.

John Glover
Feb 15, *April intro*, *July 29*, *Nov intro*.

Jacqui Hurst/Boys Syndication
Mar 1, *Mar 15*, *Apr 1*, *Apr 15*, *May intro*, *May 1*, *June 1*, *Sept intro*, *Oct 8*, *Oct 29*.

The National Trust Photographic Library
Neil Campbell-Sharp: *Nov 8*; *Marianne Majerus*: *Feb intro*; Stephen Robson: *Aug and Oct intros*.

Natural Image
Robin Fletcher: *Jan 15*; Bob Gibbons: *Jan intro*, *Jan 1*, *Mar 8*, *Mar 15*, *Mar 22*, *Mar 29*, *Apr 22*, *June 15*, *Aug 15*, *Aug 22*, *Sept 1*, *Nov 1*, *Dec 22*; Liz Gibbons: *May 29*.

The Herbal Yearbook

Written and compiled by Gillian Haslam

Colour Library Books

Planting A Herb Garden

However small or large your garden, or even if you only possess a balcony, hanging basket or window box, there is room for a herb garden. If you have enough space, you can plan the most elaborate planting schemes in the style of the formal or knot gardens of the sixteenth century. However, if you are limited to just a couple of sunny windowsills, you can still grow a year-round supply of fresh herbs to flavour your cooking, create pleasing pot pourris, scent your bath water and make into welcome gifts. All it requires is a little forethought and planning.

The first step, whether you are planting a window box or garden, is to decide which are your favourite herbs and the ones you will use most. The most popular and widely used culinary herbs are mint, basil, rosemary, thyme, chives, dill, sage and parsley. If space is at a premium, choose herbs which have several uses, for instance mint can be used in cooking, as a garnish, in various beauty preparations and dried for pot pourris.

Ideally, herb beds should be planted close to the kitchen door so that it is easy to gather the herbs required for cooking. As an alternative, however, plant up several large pots with your favourite culinary herbs and position these just outside the door. The scent will also waft indoors on warm summer days.

There are many herbs which are worth growing simply for their flowers. Marigolds and nasturtiums are two of the most cheerful herbs, producing masses of orange and yellow flowers throughout the summer. Nasturtiums are particularly good in hanging baskets and window boxes as their bright green leaves and colourful flowers will cascade down.

Some herbs produce the most fragrant scents of all garden plants. One herb that falls into this category is the ever-popular lavender. Rather than just growing the more common purple variety, experiment with plants which produce white and pink flowers – these also have a stronger scent. Dwarf species of lavender are suitable for window boxes. Other beautifully scented herbs include lemon balm, bergamot, various mints and

rosemary. Try planting a lawn of creeping thyme or chamomile – the scent will be released as you walk across it and bruise the leaves.

Many herbs have such attractive flowers that they can easily be grown in flower beds rather than in a separate herb bed. Create a country cottage-style flower border with feverfew, soapwort, chamomile, lavender, bergamot, nasturtiums, marigolds, chives and borage.

You may wish to group herbs together according to the different colours of their flowers. The following herbs have similar shades:

Yellow: tansy, feverfew, chamomile, yarrow
White: woodruff, garlic chives, some mints, lavender
Pink: chives, some mints, lavender, rosemary
Blue: borage, lavender
Red: bergamot, opal basil
Orange: nasturtium, marigold

When planning herb beds, it is important to consider the height the plants will eventually reach. Taller herbs which will provide a good backdrop at the back of the bed include bay, rosemary, tansy, sage, lovage and dill. In the middle of the bed plant medium-sized herbs, such as lavenders, mints and tarragon. Place the shorter herbs and those that provide good ground cover (and therefore less weeding!) at the front, for example chives and thyme.

It is always cheering to be able to pick fresh produce in winter, so grow a number of herbs which can provide fresh foliage to be used as flavourings or salad leaves during the winter months. Winter savory, rosemary, bay, salad burnet and French sorrel are ideal. Alternatively, you can extend the growing season of some herbs by planting them in pots which can be brought into greenhouses or conservatories when the first frosts of the autumn are forecast. This will fool the herbs into thinking it is still summer!

Before planting your herb garden, it is important to prepare the soil properly. Dig it over thoroughly, ideally before winter arrives, so that winter frosts will break up the soil and improve its texture and drainage.

Before planting the herbs, dig in some compost or manure to enrich the soil. If you are patient, buy packets of herb seeds and grow your own seedlings. Alternatively, many garden centres sell herbs and if you visit a local herb farm you will find a good selection of plants, including some of the more unusual varieties. Do not plant the herbs too close together – many of them are spreading plants and need room to grow.

Herb gardens can become quiet, peaceful places where you retreat to gather your thoughts after a hectic day. If you have room, buy a sturdy wooden garden bench and place it near a bed of scented herbs. Many herbs release their scent in the evening – what better place could there be to sit and enjoy an early evening drink.

The Language of Herbs

Since time immemorial, all types of plants, but particularly herbs and flowers, have had special meanings. In earlier centuries it became very popular to send bouquets or posies of flowers with hidden messages of love and friendship, for example a posy of thyme, mint and sorrel would convey affection.

Bay wreath	Reward of merit
Basil	Love
Balm	Sympathy
Chamomile	Energy in adversity, initiative
Coriander	Concealed merit, hidden worth
Cowslip	Pensiveness, happiness
Elder	Zealousness
Fennel	Force and strength
Garden sage	Esteem
Hop	Injustice
Hyssop	Cleanliness
Lavender	Distrust; sweets to the sweet
Marigold	Despair, grief; honesty
Marjoram	Blushes
Mint	Virtue
Nasturtium	Patriotism, optimism, splendour
Parsley	Feasting, festivity; useful knowledge
Pennyroyal	Flee away
Peppermint	Cordiality
Rocket	Rivalry
Rosemary	Remembrance; your presence revives me
Sage	Domestic virtue, wisdom
Sorrel	Affection
Southernwood	Bantering, jest
Spearmint	Warmth of sentiment
Sweet basil	Good wishes
Thyme	Energy, affection
Verbena	You have my confidence

Harvesting and Drying Herbs

In the past, before the days of advanced farming techniques and imported fruits and vegetables, drying herbs was one of the few ways to preserve the flavours of summer for the coming winter months. Although it is usually far better to use fresh rather than dried herbs in cooking, this is normally only possible during summer. The next best option is to harvest and dry the herbs. As well as being used in cooking, dried herbs can also be used in pot pourri, as fillings for scented sachets and infused to make teas and tisanes.

Most herbs should be harvested just as they come into flower and before the seeds form, as they will be at their best then. Gather the herbs in the morning as soon as the dew has evaporated and before they begin to wilt in the heat of the day. Discard any old or discoloured leaves.

Herbs need to be dried as quickly as possible in order to preserve their flavour and colour. However, drying them in direct sunlight will damage them. They can be dried in several different ways. Individual leaves can be placed on trays covered with absorbent kitchen paper and left in a warm, dry place away from direct sunlight, such as an airing cupboard.

Alternatively, heat the oven on its lowest setting and place the herbs inside to dry. Check the leaves regularly to make sure they do not burn.

One of the prettiest and more traditional ways to dry them is to pick herbs with fairly long stems, strip the lower leaves from the stems and group them into bunches. Tie the stems together with a long length of string and hang the bunches upside down in a warm place to dry. The bunches look very attractive hanging in the kitchen above the stove. When the leaves are completely dry, strip them from the stalks and store them in screwtop jars or cloth bags. Store in a dark place. Do not crumble the leaves until just before you want to use them as this will help preserve the flavour.

One of the quickest ways to dry herbs is to use the microwave. Strip the leaves from the stems and place them in a single layer on a sheet of absorbent kitchen paper. Cook on HIGH for 1 minute, then turn the leaves over and cook for a further 1-1½ minutes until they are completely dry.

Fresh herbs can also be frozen, although the majority of herbs become rather limp when thawed. Wash the herbs

and dry them thoroughly. Tie them into small bunches and place in polythene bags. Seal the bags to make them airtight and place in the freezer. When required, the frozen bunches of herbs can be add directly to casseroles and soups. If you wish, herbs such as parsley can be crumbled while still frozen.

If you wish to dry herb flowers, you must pick them carefully to avoid damaging the petals. Choose flowers with long stems and tie them together in bunches. Hang them upside down in a warm place and leave to dry. If the flowers do not have long stems, place the flowers carefully on a wire cooling rack so the air can circulate around them, and leave in a warm, dry place.

To dry herb seeds, cut the seedheads from the plant just as they begin to turn brown. Place the seedheads in large paper bags and leave to dry in a warm room. As the seeds dry, they will fall out of the seedhead to the bottom of the paper bag. Store the seeds in glass jars out of direct light.

January

Borage

Borage (*Borago officinalis*) is one of the prettiest herbs to grow, with its abundant sky blue or pink star-shaped flowers with distinctive black centres. It is an annual herb and grows quickly from seed to become a large, sprawling plant, reaching a height of 45-75 cm (18-30 in), so make sure you grow it where there is plenty of space. It is not suitable for container growing due to its long tap root. Either leave the plant to seed itself or sow seeds in spring and autumn.

Although it does not transplant very well, borage will thrive in a poor chalky or sandy soil with plenty of sun. It is quite a hardy plant and will continue to bloom for many months, whatever the weather. The borage plant has tough, prickly green leaves which, when young, are a good source of vitamin C and can be cooked like spinach.

In herbal medicine infusions of borage are used to treat colds, bronchitis and rheumatic conditions and in compresses to treat skin rashes.

Both the leaves and flowers of the borage plant smell and taste remarkably like cucumber, which is why they are often added to iced drinks. Add flowers and finely chopped leaves to pitchers of Pimms, fruit punches or wine cups.

January

1

2

3

In medieval times borage was thought to provide courage. The Crusaders were said to drink infusions of borage leaves mixed with wine before heading into battle.

4

5

'Sprigs of borage are of known virtue to revive the hypochondriac and cheer the hard student.'

John Evelyn, late seventeenth century

6

7

Herb Ice Bowl

An ice bowl is a stunning centrepiece for a dinner party. It is easy to make and can be filled with a fresh fruit salad (as shown in the photograph), ice cream, sorbets or iced soup. Here the ice bowl has been decorated with fresh nasturtiums, borage flowers, mint leaves and chamomile blossoms. Make sure you stand the ice bowl on a large dinner plate to catch the drips as it slowly melts.

1 Use two glass freezerproof bowls which, when fitted one inside the other, leave a gap of about 2.5 cm (1 in) between them. Fill the larger bowl with cold water to a depth of about 4 cm (1½ in) and add a handful of fresh herb flowers and leaves. Place carefully in the freezer, ensuring the bowl is level, and leave until frozen.

2 Place the smaller bowl on top of the frozen layer of water and weigh it down by placing a heavy weight inside the smaller bowl. Fill the gap between the two bowls with cold water and add more flowers and leaves. Make sure these are pushed well down in the water to decorate the sides of the bowl. Return to freezer until frozen.

3 To release the ice bowl, wipe the inside of the smaller bowl with a cloth wrung out in hot water and twist the bowl gently to loosen. To remove the larger bowl, dip in tepid water and twist to loosen. Return the ice bowl to the freezer until ready to use.

Borage Face Mask

This revitalising face mask is suitable for dry skins. Place a handful of clean, young borage leaves in a blender with 1 tbsp water and purée to a pulp. Mix in enough sour cream to form a paste. Apply to clean, damp skin. Relax for 15 minutes, then wash the mask off with warm water.

Peppermint

Peppermint (Mentha piperita) is a hybrid of spearmint and water mint. It has deep red stems, red-tinged long leaves and small, violet coloured flowers. This is the strongest of all the mint varieties, containing the most menthol, and it is widely grown on a commercial basis for a variety of medicinal and cosmetic uses, such as toothpaste. It is used as a flavouring in confectionery, such as after-dinner mints and chocolates, and is also known as brandy mint because it is the mint used in crème de menthe. Its leaves make a refreshing herbal tea. It is often grown for its oil and is one of the most important essential oils.

Peppermint thrives in a fairly warm, moist climate and prefers open textured, well drained soils. It is fairly resistant to garden pests, although it can be damaged by caterpillars and grasshoppers.

Peppermint Tea

Peppermint makes a refreshing herbal tea and also aids digestion. Add three teaspoons of crushed fresh leaves to one pot of boiling water and leave to infuse for three to four minutes. If necessary, sweeten with a teaspoonful of honey.

Peppermint milk makes a good nightcap. Pour 300 ml (½ pint) of boiling milk over three teaspoons of crushed mint leaves.

January

8

9

10

Rats dislike peppermint. When clearing a building of rats, rat-catchers block up many of the rodents' escape exits with rags soaked in oil of peppermint.

11

12

13

14

Herb Jellies

Makes about 450 g (1 lb)

Herb jellies are extremely useful to keep in the kitchen storecupboard, and they make welcome gifts. Top the jam jars with a pretty circle of fabric for an old-fashioned, country look. Sage jelly goes well with roast game, while rosemary jelly is a good accompaniment to cold ham. Serve mint jelly with roast lamb, to make a change from the more traditional mint sauce. Make sure the jam jars are completely clean and have been warmed before filling them with the jelly.

1.4-1.8 kg (3-4 lb) cooking apples, washed and quartered
Granulated or preserving sugar
Juice of 1 lemon
Selection of fresh, chopped herbs (such as rosemary, mint, chives, sage, thyme)
Green food colouring (optional)

1 Place the prepared apples in a large saucepan with enough water to cover them. Slowly bring the water to the boil and then simmer for 1 hour. Stir the fruit gently several times while cooking.

2 Remove the pan from the heat and allow it to cool slightly. Suspend a jelly bag or muslin cloth over a large bowl. Pour the apples and their juice into the bag and leave to drip for several hours. Do not squeeze the juice from the bag or the jelly will go cloudy.

3 Measure the juice and pour into a large saucepan. Bring to the boil. For every 600 ml (1 pint) of juice, add 450 g (1 lb) of warm sugar. Stir over a medium heat until the sugar has dissolved.

4 Boil the jelly until it reaches a setting point of 105°C (220°F). Add the lemon juice to the pan and remove from the heat. If you wish to colour the jelly green, add a couple of drops of food colouring.

5 Pour the jelly into hot, dry jars and stir in the herbs of your choice. The jelly sets rapidly so you will need to work quickly. Seal and label the jars.

Courgette and Peppermint Soup

Serves 4

The addition of fresh peppermint gives this recipe a sharper taste. If you wish, serve the soup garnished with fresh peppermint leaves and a swirl of double cream.

15 ml (1 tbsp) oil
1 medium onion, peeled and finely chopped
1 small clove garlic, peeled and crushed
2 medium potatoes, peeled and diced
675 g (1½ lb) courgettes, finely sliced
1.2 litres (2 pints) hot chicken stock
Salt and freshly ground black pepper
2 eggs
1 tbsp grated Parmesan cheese
1 tbsp chopped fresh peppermint
Pinch of nutmeg

1 Put the oil, onion and garlic in a large bowl. Cook in the microwave, uncovered, on HIGH for 2-3 minutes to soften, then add the potatoes and cook on HIGH for 2 minutes. Stir in the courgettes and cook on HIGH for 3-4 minutes.

2 Stir in the stock, salt and pepper, cover and cook on HIGH for 5-15 minutes until the vegetables are soft. Pour into a food processor or blender, purée and then return the liquid to the bowl.

3 Beat the eggs, cheese, peppermint and nutmeg together. Gradually add to the soup, whisking continuously. Cook, uncovered, on HIGH for 3-5 minutes or until hot, stirring once.

Marjoram

Marjoram is a sweetly scented herb often found in Mediterranean cookery. It grows as a small bush with tiny green leaves and pink flowers. There are three main varieties of marjoram. Pot marjoram (Origanum onites) is a hardy plant which grows well in colder climates. It has a strong flavour and is used in many dishes from Greece, where it can be found growing wild.

Knotted or sweet marjoram (Origanum majorana) is used a lot in French cuisine. It has a more delicate flavour and should be added towards the end of the cooking time so that it does not lose its flavour.

The third marjoram is known as oregano (Origanum vulgare), also called wild marjoram. It is the strongest of the three varieties and is used mainly in Italian cookery.

January

15

16

'Indeed, sir, she was the sweet Marjoram of the Salad, or rather, the Herb-of-Grace.'

All's Well that Ends Well
William Shakespeare

17

18

Dried and ground marjoram was used as snuff in times gone by.

19

20

Folklore has it that if marjoram and wild thyme are laid near milk in a dairy, they will prevent it being turned by thunder.

21

Swordfish Kebabs

Serves 4-5

Swordfish is one of the most commonly caught fish in the Mediterranean, especially in Italy. It is a firm fish and the flesh will not fall apart during cooking – essential when making kebabs. Fresh tuna may be used instead. Serve the kebabs with rice and a fresh green salad.

1 kg (2¼ lb) swordfish steaks
90 ml (6 tbsp) olive oil
1 tsp chopped oregano
1 tsp chopped marjoram
Juice and rind of ½ lemon
Cherry tomatoes
2 lemons, cut into thin slices
Salt and freshly ground black pepper
Parsley, to garnish

1 Cut the swordfish steaks into 5 cm (2 inch) cubes.

2 Mix the olive oil, herbs, lemon juice and rind together and set aside. Thread the swordfish, tomatoes and lemon slices on to skewers, alternating the ingredients.

3 Brush the skewers with the oil and lemon mixture and cook under a pre-heated grill for about 10 minutes, turning occasionally and basting frequently with the oil and lemon mixture. Serve garnished with parsley.

Perfect Pizzas

Pizzas originate from the Italian city of Naples where they have been a staple part of the diet for hundreds of years. From their early, humble beginnings, pizzas have now become everyday meals the world over, with many restaurants producing their own special combination of ingredients to top the pizza dough. It often seems that the best toppings are the simplest. Piling on too many ingredients means the different flavours can cancel each other out.

One of the oldest and most authentic Italian toppings is a simple mixture of oil, tomatoes, salt and pepper, crushed garlic and a generous sprinkling of oregano.

Marjoram oil is said to relieve toothache. It takes over 200 lb of marjoram to produce just 1 lb of oil. Herbs for oil extraction should be gathered when just coming into flower.

Pennyroyal

Pennyroyal (Mentha pulegium) is quite unlike any other varieties of the mint family. Rather than producing a bushy plant, it grows as a low-lying, creeping half-hardy perennial, making it ideal ground cover. Due to its growing habits, its country names include 'Run-by-the-ground' and 'Lurk-in-the-ditch'. It will grow in any type of soil but prefers moist conditions. During its growing season it produces clusters of mauve flowers. It is one of the mints ideal for growing in containers or window boxes as it need not take up too much space. It has a strong flavour and smell so should only be used sparingly in cookery.

Pennyroyal was said to be good for treating headaches. An old herbal states: 'A garland of pennyroyal made and worn about the head is of great force against the swimming in the head and the pains and giddiness thereof.'

Pennyroyal Pot Pourri

Pennyroyal is excellent when dried and used in pot pourris. Its scent is ideal mixed with lavender for a simple green and mauve mixture. If the scent is not strong enough or begins to fade, add a few drops of lavender essential oil.

January

22

23

24

Years ago pennyroyal was grown in pots and carried on long sea voyages. It was used by sailors to purify casks of drinking water.

25

26

27

28

A pot of pennyroyal grown indoors should keep away mosquitoes and fleas.

Pea Soup with Mint

Serves 6-8

Served with crusty French bread, this makes an ideal lunch or supper dish. If mint is unavailable, substitute other fresh herbs, such as marjoram, chervil or thyme. Dried split peas are readily available in supermarkets and health food stores.

180 g (6 oz) dried split peas
560 g (1¼ lb) frozen peas
90 g (3 oz) fresh mint leaves
120 g (4 oz) butter or margarine, melted
Pinch of salt and pepper
Sprigs of fresh mint, to garnish

1 Place the split peas in a saucepan with about 1.7 litres (3 pints) of water. Cover, bring to the boil and cook for about 40 minutes until very tender.

2 Strain the peas and reserve the liquid.

3 Pour the liquid back into the saucepan and add the frozen peas. Chop the mint leaves, reserving some for the garnish, and add to the saucepan. Cover and bring to the boil.

4 Meanwhile, add the melted butter or margarine to the split peas and push through a strainer or work in a food processor to form a smooth purée. Add the purée to the saucepan, mixing well. Add salt and pepper to taste.

5 Pour the hot soup into a tureen, garnish with mint sprigs and serve immediately.

Herb Croûtons

Croûtons make an excellent garnish for salads and soups. Store them in an airtight tin for freshness. For garlic and herb croûtons, add some crushed garlic to the frying pan.

1 Cut day-old or stale bread into small cubes or small shapes using fancy pastry cutters.

2 Melt equal quantities of butter and oil in a frying pan and fry the bread shapes until golden.

3 Meanwhile, place some finely chopped fresh herbs in a paper bag. When the croûtons are cooked and still hot, place them in the paper bag and shake until they are coated with herbs.

Chamomile

Chamomile (Matricaria chamomilla) is an annual herb with small, scented yellow and white flowers. It is very easy to grow from seeds sown in early spring. If the flowers are left to go to seed, the plant will come up year after year. Chamomile prefers a dry, sunny position and light, well drained soil, and will also grow well in containers.

Chamomile has a great many healing and cosmetic uses. In Ancient Egypt it was dedicated to the gods and revered for its medicinal powers. A simple infusion of chamomile flowers makes a good herbal rinse for fair hair, and among its many other uses are mouthwashes and eyebaths. Its oil is widely used in the pharmaceutical industry.

Another fragrant plant in the same botanical family is Roman chamomile (Anthemis nobilis). This is a dwarf species used when planting scented chamomile lawns.

Chamomile Tea

Chamomile makes a soothing tea to settle indigestion and stomach upsets or for those who have difficulty sleeping. It has a slightly bitter taste and a delicate aroma. It can be made from either fresh or dried flowers. Infuse the flowers in hot water for three or four minutes and add a teaspoon of honey to sweeten the tea, if desired.

January

29

30

31

Natural Dyeing with Chamomile and Marigold Flowers

Dried chamomile and marigold flowers are two herbs which can be used for dyeing natural fibres such as wool or fabric. They produce pleasant pastel shades of cream and yellow. If using chamomile flowers, use the same weight of flowers as the weight of material to be dyed. If dyeing with marigolds, allow twice the weight of flowers to the weight of material.

You will need:

450 g (1 lb) dried chamomile flower heads or 900 g (2 lb) dried marigold flower heads
450 g (1 lb) clean sheep's wool or cotton fabric
75 g (3 oz) alum (potassium aluminium sulphate)
25 g (1 oz) cream of tartar
Large enamel or stainless steel dye pan or saucepan
Rubber gloves

1 Dissolve the alum and cream of tartar in the pan in enough water to cover the fabric or wool. Add the fabric or wool when the water is warm and heat slowly until the water is boiling.

2 Reduce heat and simmer for 45 minutes. This process is called mordanting and is necessary to fix the natural dye already in the fabric.

3 Drain the wool or fabric from the pan and set aside. Discard the mordant.

4 Put the flowers in the pan and add approximately 4.5 litres (1 gallon) cold water. Bring to the boil and simmer for 1 hour.

5 Strain off the flower heads and add the mordanted wool or fabric to the liquid dye. Bring to the boil, then simmer for 1 hour or until the desired colour is reached. The longer the fabric is boiled, the more colour it will absorb.

6 Remove fabric or wool from the pan, rinse gently in cold water and hang out to dry. Hand-washing is recommended thereafter in case the colour runs.

Chamomile Facial Steam

Facial steams are ideal for brightening up dull, tired skin; however they are not recommended for particularly dry skin.

First cleanse your face thoroughly to remove any dirt and grime. Place a handful of chamomile flowers in a bowl of boiling water. Hold your face about 30 cm (12 in) above the bowl and cover your head with a towel to prevent the steam escaping. Steam your face for about 10 minutes, then refresh the skin with a clean, damp face cloth.

Other herbs suitable for this are marigolds, peppermint, sage, comfrey and fennel.

February

Angelica

Angelica (Angelica archangelica) is a large biennial herb with glossy green leaves and self-seeding white flowers which bloom from midsummer. It is a hardy plant which can grow to a height of 1-2 m (3-6 ft). It thrives in colder, northern climates, growing well in rich soil and partially shaded areas. Its tiny flowers are gathered into one large umbel and its large leaves are divided into small leaflets arranged in groups of three.

Nowadays angelica is best known in its candied form, with the bright green stems used to decorate cakes and trifles, but in the past all parts of the herb were used. The sweet leaves can be added to preserves or fruit dishes, or dried and used as a tension-reducing tisane. The leaf stalks can be cooked with gooseberries or rhubarb to reduce acidity, while the roots and stems can be cooked and eaten as a vegetable.

The taste of angelica is similar to that of juniper and, like juniper, the oils made from its leaves, roots and seeds are used to flavour gin and liqueurs.

February

1

Angelica is said to protect against evil spirits and witchcraft; for that reason it is known as 'The Root of the Holy Ghost'.

2

3

4

5

6

According to folklore, angelica takes its name from the archangel who recommended its use in times of plague.

7

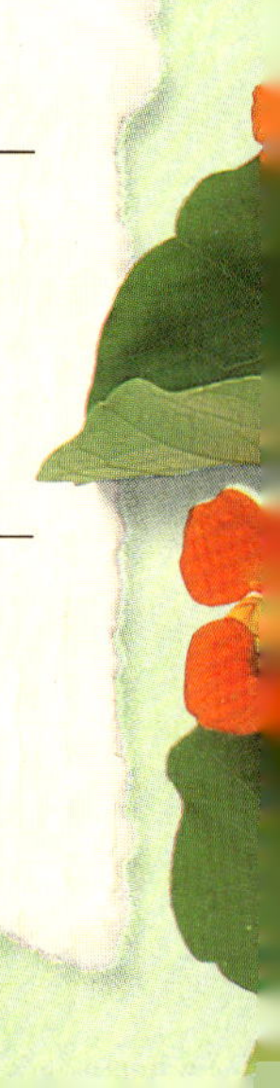

Needlepoint Sleep Pillow

This needlepoint cushion is filled with a mixture of dried herb with sleep-inducing properties. Make the cushion as large or as small as you wish simply by increasing or reducing the size of the border surrounding the central nasturtium design.

You will need:

10-mesh double thread needlepoint canvas
Oddments of tapestry wools in various shades of red, orange, yellow and green
Blunt-ended tapestry needle
Masking tape
Small piece of fabric for backing
Wadding
Small muslin remnant
Mixture of dried herbs (such as hops, lavender, mint)

1 Bind the four edges of the canvas with masking tape to prevent the canvas fraying.

2 Mark the centre of the canvas and stitch the innermost orange border. Each side of the border here is 31 stitches. Work in tent stitch using a single thread. When starting a new colour, leave a 2.5 cm (1 in) loose end on the wrong side; catch the loose end under the first few stitches to secure it.

3 Following the pattern shown in the detail photograph, stitch the central nasturtium design. Use short lengths of tapestry wool and do not carry long lengths of yarn across the back of the cushion. When the nasturtium is finished, fill in the green and cream dot background.

4 Stitch the yellow and orange borders and then work the remaining background and border.

5 Remove the masking tape and, right sides facing, sew the canvas to the backing fabric on three sides.

6 Turn the cushion right sides out. Make a small sachet from the muslin remnant and fill with the herb mixture. Place this inside the cushion with the wadding.

7 Sew the remaining edges together with coordinating thread and small, neat stitches.

Candied Angelica

Bright green candied angelica is the perfect ingredient for decorating cakes and trifles and for adding to rich fruit cakes.

1 Cut narrow, young stems of angelica into 6 cm (2½ in) lengths. Wash well and then cook in a saucepan of boiling water until tender. Drain well and peel off any tough outer skin.

2 Weigh the cooked angelica and measure out an equal amount of caster sugar. Layer the angelica and the sugar in a dish, cover and leave for 1-2 days until the sugar has liquified.

3 Place the sugar and angelica in a saucepan and heat gently until the liquid has nearly evaporated.

4 Remove the angelica and place on a wire rack. Leave in a warm place for a couple of days until dry. Pack the candied angelica in an airtight jar until required.

Woodruff

Woodruff (Asperula odorata) is a pretty, delicate herb often found growing wild in woods and shaded hedgerows. It can easily be recognised by its small white flowers which bloom in early summer and its narrow leaves which grow in star-shaped formations. It is a low-growing plant, rarely reaching more than 20 cm (8 in) in height.

Woodruff is rarely cultivated, but usually seeds itself. Its seeds form a small ball covered with bristles which attach themselves to the fur and feathers of animals or birds, thereby dispersing the seeds. In the past it was often used for pharmaceutical purposes as its fragrance could disguise any unpleasant odours from other chemicals.

During the Middle Ages woodruff was often used in herbal medicine. It was said to be useful in treating liver conditions and its fresh, bruised leaves were reported to heal cuts and wounds.

In Germany a traditional drink known as Maibowle was made by steeping sprigs of woodruff in wine from the Rhine vineyards.

February

8

9

Dried woodruff can be stored in sachets in linen cupboards to deter insects.

10

11

Powdered woodruff leaves can be mixed with snuff to add a pleasant fragrance.

12

13

14

Stir-Fried Vegetables with Herbs

Serves 6

These crisply cooked vegetables flavoured with herbs make a perfect side dish. Either serve them hot to accompany a meat dish or cold as a salad.

4 sticks of celery
4 medium courgettes
2 red peppers, seeded
30-45 ml (3-4 tbsp) oil
Pinch of salt and pepper
5 ml (1 tsp) fresh oregano or marjoram, chopped
60 ml (4 tbsp) snipped fresh chives

1 Slice the celery diagonally into pieces about 1.25 cm (½ in) thick.

2 Cut the courgettes in half lengthways and then cut into 1.25 cm (½ in) thick slices.

3 Cut the pepper into strips and then into 2.5 cm (1 in) diagonal pieces.

4 Heat the oil in a heavy frying pan over a medium heat. Add the celery and stir-fry until just tender.

5 Add the courgettes and pepper and stir-fry until all the vegetables are tender but still crisp.

6 Add the salt, pepper and oregano or marjoram and cook for a further 30 seconds. Stir in the chives and serve.

Mixed Pepper Relish

Makes 1 litre (2 pints)

Prepare this tangy relish with a mixture of different coloured peppers. Serve as an accompaniment to cheese, egg and meat dishes. It also complements fish and shellfish.

1.5 kg (3 lb) peppers, seeded
2 medium onions, finely chopped
2.5 ml (½ tsp) oregano
2.5 ml (½ tsp) coriander
2 bay leaves
Salt, to taste
450 g (1 lb) granulated or preserving sugar
430 ml (¾ pint) white wine vinegar or white distilled vinegar

1 Cut the peppers into small dice and combine with the onions in a large saucepan.

2 Pour over boiling water to cover and return to the boil. Cook rapidly for 10 minutes and drain well.

3 Meanwhile, combine the sugar and vinegar in a large saucepan. Bring slowly to the boil to dissolve the sugar, stirring occasionally.

4 Add the drained peppers and onions and the herbs to the vinegar and sugar. Bring back to the boil and then simmer for 30 minutes.

5 Meanwhile, sterilise the jars by placing them in a saucepan of boiling water and boiling them for 15 minutes. Remove the jars from the water and drain.

6 Remove the bay leaves and pour the relish into warm, sterilised jars and seal.

Purple Sage

Purple sage (*Salvia purpurascens*) is very similar to the more common green sage. This variety comes in different shades, from green leaves with a purple underside through to a very dark, almost black variety. This is another herb native to the Mediterranean area where it is still widely used in cookery. It generally grows to about 30 cm (1 foot) in height and is fairly hardy, so it can withstand wintry weather. It can be quite shrubby in appearance with a spicy fragrance and in late summer produces purplish flowers.

Its botanical name comes from the Latin *salvere*, meaning to save. This refers to its many medicinal properties. It can be used as a mouthwash to relieve sore throats and inflamed gums and it was considered a useful medicine for treating everything from typhoid fever to liver complaints, from measles to general lethargy.

Sage infusions were used to heal skin abrasions and as a lotion for ulcers.

February

15

Fresh sage leaves, rubbed on the teeth, will clean them and strengthen the gums.

16

17

Dried sage leaves were once smoked in pipes as a cure for asthma.

18

19

20

21

In southern England years ago, eating sage leaves on nine consecutive mornings, whilst fasting, was believed to be a cure for ague.

Red Mullet with Herb and Mushroom Sauce

Ask your fishmonger to gut the fish, scale them and remove the gills for you. If red mullet is not available, use other fish such as bream or sardines. Serve this Italian dish with a simple crisp green salad.

450 g (1 lb) small mushrooms, left whole
1 clove garlic, finely chopped
45 ml (3 tbsp) olive oil
Juice of 1 lemon
15 ml (1 tbsp) finely chopped parsley
10 ml (2 tsp) finely chopped basil
5 ml (1 tsp) finely chopped sage
60 ml (4 tbsp) dry white wine mixed with 2.5 ml (½ tsp) cornflour
Few drops of anchovy essence
4 red mullet, each weighing about 225 g (8 oz), cleaned and prepared
10 ml (2 tsp) white breadcrumbs
10 ml (2 tsp) freshly grated Parmesan cheese

1 Combine the mushrooms, garlic and oil in a small frying pan. Cook over a moderate heat for about 1 minute until the garlic and mushrooms are slightly softened. Add all the herbs, lemon juice and white wine and cornflour mixture. Bring to the boil and cook until thickened. Add anchovy essence to taste.

2 Rinse the fish and pat dry. Place the fish head to tail in a shallow ovenproof dish that can be used for serving. The fish should fit snugly into the dish.

3 Pour the sauce over the fish and sprinkle with breadcrumbs and Parmesan cheese.

4 Cover the dish loosely with foil and cook in an oven pre-heated to 190°C/375° F/gas mark 5 for about 20 minutes. Uncover for the last 5 minutes, if desired, and raise the temperature slightly to brown the fish.

Sage Varieties

Sage is available in a variety of different colours, from the purple variety shown here, to pale grey-green plants, yellow and green variegated leaves and a tricolour variety of green leaves speckled with pink, purple and cream. All the varieties have slightly different flavours, and there is also a pineapple-flavoured sage. If you use a lot of sage in cooking, try growing a pot of mixed varieties just outside the kitchen door.

An infusion of sage massaged onto the scalp will darken the hair and disguise grey hairs. Make a strong infusion of about 4 tablespoons of leaves to one cup of water and apply to the roots every day. To increase the darkening effect, mix the sage with tea instead of water.

Rocket

Rocket (*Eruca sativa*) is a strongly flavoured herb often used in salads, with a taste resembling cress. A native of the Mediterranean region, it is a half-hardy annual with long, green leaves and creamy-white flowers. It will thrive in moist soil and either sun or partial shade. Rocket can be grown from seed sown in autumn or spring. It is well worth growing as it is ready for harvesting within eight weeks. The leaves can be cooked like spinach.

In the language of herbs rocket means deceit, as it has a lovely perfume in the evening but during the day is unscented. It is also known by the names Dame's Violet, Dame's Rocket and Vesper Flower (due to its evening scent).

February

22

'Excellent herbs had our fathers of old
Excellent herbs to ease their pain.'

Rudyard Kipling

23

24

25

26

Rocket leaves should be gathered before the plant is in flower.

27

28/29

Mixed Herb Sauce

Makes 175 ml (6 fl oz)

This sauce is extremely easy to make and can be flavoured with whatever fresh herbs you have to hand. Parsley, thyme and basil work particularly well together. Serve the sauce with cold meats or salads.

175 ml (6 fl oz) olive oil
30 ml (2 tbsp) lemon juice
3 tbsp chopped fresh herbs
2 drops Tabasco sauce
Salt and freshly ground black pepper

Combine all the ingredients, apart from the salt and pepper, in a food processor or blender and mix well. Season to taste and pour into a serving jug. The sauce can be stored in the refrigerator for up to 3 days.

Herb Butters

These two butters are very easy to make and add a pretty, decorative touch to a dinner party. They freeze well so can be made in advance. The slices can be used to top grilled fish or meat, cooked vegetables or corn on the cob, or with a cheese board at the end of the meal.

1 Take a handful of finely chopped fresh herbs (such as parsley or coriander) and mix with slightly softened butter. Pack tightly into ramekins or individual butter crocks and refrigerate until required. Garnish the top of the butters with a sprig of herbs. Alternatively, pack into decorative butter moulds and chill, or roll a teaspoon of the herb butter between ribbed wooden butter paddles to make butter balls with fluted edges.

2 Finely chop a small handful of nasturtium blossoms and mix in a bowl with slightly softened butter. On a piece of plastic wrap shape the butter into a sausage shape. Wrap tightly in the plastic wrap and refrigerate. When required, carefully unwrap from the plastic and cut the butter into slices.

March

Sorrel

Sorrel (*Rumex acetosa*) belongs to the dock family, native to Europe. It is very similar to spinach, both in appearance and taste and in cooking methods. It is often used in a sauce to accompany fish, in tarts and soups, and the young leaves can be eaten raw in salads. In spring the leaves are almost tasteless, but develop an acidity as the summer progresses.

Sorrel will grow in most types of soil and situations. It will grow to about 60 cm (2 ft) in height, producing reddish-green flowers in midsummer. Its green leaves are oblong in shape and the lower leaves grow to about 15 cm (6 in) in length.

Although mainly grown for culinary use, sorrel does possess medicinal properties. A syrup made with sorrel and vinegar was used as a gargle to soothe sore throats, and a decoction of flowers and wine was said to cure jaundice.

Herb Soaps

There are many ancient recipes for using herbs to scent soaps. Infusions can be made with various scented leaves or flowers, or a few drops of essential oils can be added to soaps while in their liquid stage. If using essential oils, remember they are very strong and just a few drops will suffice.

March

1

2

Sorrel is also known by its country names of Cuckoo Sorrow, Sour Sabs, Sour Suds and Green Sauce.

3

4

5

6

The root and the seed of sorrel were once valued for their astringent properties.

7

Sorrel Sauce

Sorrel sauce is an excellent accompaniment to poached white fish and salmon. It also goes well with pasta. When preparing sorrel, cut out the central stalk which can be rather tough.

100 g (4 oz) sorrel, chopped
300 ml (½ pint) fish or chicken stock
15 g (½ oz) butter
1 tbsp flour
4 tbsp cream
salt and freshly ground black pepper

1 Simmer the sorrel leaves in the stock for 5 minutes. Allow to cool slightly, then purée in a blender or food processor.

2 Melt the butter in a saucepan, add the flour and stir over a gentle heat until blended.

3 Add the sorrel purée to the saucepan and simmer for 4 minutes, stirring. Add the cream and season to taste. Serve immediately.

Liquid Lavender Soap

6 tbsp castile soap, grated
600 ml (1 pint) water
5 tbsp glycerine
4 drops of lavender oil
Natural food colouring (optional)

Put the soap and water in a heatproof bowl and place over a saucepan of boiling water. When the soap has melted, stir in the glycerine. Remove from the heat and stir in the lavender oil. If desired, stir in a few drops of natural food colouring to colour the soap. When cool, pour into clean bottles and seal with corks.

Marigold Soap

2 tbsp fresh marigold petals, finely chopped
2 tbsp glycerine, warmed
12 tbsp castile soap, grated
1 tbsp clear honey
Natural food colouring (optional)

Place the chopped marigold petals in the warmed glycerine and leave to infuse in a warm place for 2 hours. Melt the soap in a heatproof bowl placed over a saucepan of boiling water. Remove from the heat and add the glycerine infusion, honey and food colouring, if wanted. Pour the soap into glycerine-greased moulds and leave to set.

Rosemary

Rosemary (Rosemarinus officinalis) is a strong flavoured, hardy evergreen herb. With its aromatic, needle-shaped, blue-green leaves, it is easily identified. Silver and gold-striped varieties are also available. In late spring and during mild weather it produces blue, white or pink flowers.

This herb grows best in light, dry soil and prefers a sheltered position. It is more fragrant if grown on a chalky soil.

Rosemary is said to thrive in households where 'the mistress, not the master, rules'! Rosemary shrubs can be found growing wild in the Mediterranean and its distinctive flavour can be tasted in the cooking of Provence, Italy and Spain. The leaves should be finely chopped for use in cooking. Alternatively, whole sprigs of rosemary can be laid on meats to be roasted or grilled, or added to soups and casseroles. Remember to remove the sprigs before serving.

March

8

9

A few slices of bread and home-made lard, flavoured with rosemary, and plenty of green food 'went down good' as they used to say.

Lark Rise to Candleford
Flora Thompson

10

11

Rosemary is the herb of remembrance, and sprigs are often carried at country funerals or woven into wreaths.

12

13

There's Rosemary, that's for remembrance;
Pray you love, remember.

Hamlet
William Shakespeare

14

Historically rosemary is associated with the Virgin Mary. There are two slightly different legends. According to one, rosemary flowers are supposed to have taken their colour from her blue cloak when she laid it over a rosemary bush to dry. The other story relates how rosemary bushes suddenly bloomed when Mary spread Christ's clothes on them to dry in the sun.

Spiced Lamb

Serves 4

This tender, sautéed lamb is cooked in a sauce fragrant with herbs and spices. Serve with rice or sauté potatoes and a green vegetable such as mangetout. This dish tastes just as good if pork fillet or steak are used instead of lamb.

450 g (1 lb) lamb neck fillet
5 ml (1 tsp) fresh dill, chopped
5 ml (1 tsp) rosemary, crushed
5 ml (1 tsp) thyme, chopped
10 ml (2 tsp) mustard seeds, slightly crushed
2 bay leaves
5 ml (1 tsp) coarsely ground black pepper
2.5 ml (½ tsp) ground allspice
Juice of 2 lemons
280 ml (½ pint) red wine
30 ml (2 tbsp) oil
30 g (2 tbsp) butter or margarine
1 small red pepper, seeded and sliced
90 g (3 oz) whole button mushrooms
45 g (3 tbsp) flour
140 ml (¼ pint) beef stock
Salt

1 Place the lamb in a shallow dish and sprinkle on the dill, rosemary, thyme and mustard seeds. Add the bay leaves, pepper, allspice, lemon juice and wine, and stir to coat the meat thoroughly with the marinade. Leave for 4 hours in the refrigerator.

2 Heat the oil in a large frying pan and add the red pepper and mushrooms and cook to soften slightly. Remove with a draining spoon.

3 Reheat the oil in the pain and add the lamb fillet, well drained and patted dry. Reserve the marinade. Brown the meat quickly on all sides to seal. Remove from the pan and set aside with the vegetables.

4 Melt the butter in the pan and, when foaming, add the flour. Lower the heat and cook the flour slowly until a good rich brown. Pour in the beef stock and the marinade. Bring to the boil and return the vegetables and lamb to the pan. Cook for about 15 minutes, or until the lamb is tender but still pink inside.

5 Slice the lamb fillet thinly on the diagonal and arrange on warmed plates. Remove the bay leaves from the sauce and spoon over the meat to serve.

Rosemary Hair Rinse

This hair rinse is extremely quick to make. Keep a bottle in your bathroom and use it as a final rinse after shampooing your hair. Rosemary hair rinse will bring out the shine in dark hair. To make a rinse for fair hair, simply replace the rosemary with chamomile flowers.

Infuse a few stalks of rosemary in hot water for several minutes. Strain the liquid, allow to cool and bottle.

Common Thyme

Common thyme (Thymus vulgaris), also known as garden thyme, is a cultivated form of the wild thyme which grows in mountainous regions of Mediterranean countries. This aromatic variety is a spreading, evergreen perennial which grows to a maximum height of about 23 cm (9 in) and which produces small mauve flowers in summer. As soon as the flowers have finished blooming, the plant should be trimmed to encourage new growth.

It prefers a sunny position and will grow on any well drained soil. The leaves' fragrance is due to thyme's essential oil, which is valued for both culinary and medicinal purposes. Its oil has been used to treat rheumatism, pounded thyme leaves mixed with a syrup are believed to help cure whooping cough, thyme tea will aid a fever, and it is said to have been used to heal leprosy. The oil is also used extensively by commercial manufacturers for scenting soap.

March

15

16

17

Thyme was used by the Romans to add an aromatic flavour to cheeses and liqueurs.

18

19

20

21

A Carpet of Thyme

If you have room in your garden, try planting a thyme lawn. Choose a selection of creeping thymes with different coloured foliage and flowers and plant close to each other so that they form a spreading multi-coloured carpet. Suitable varieties include Wooley thyme, which has bright pink flowers, silver thyme, golden-tipped thyme, lemon thyme or E B Anderson thyme, which is a mixture of gold and green colouring.

Scampi Provençale

Serves 4

This microwave version of a classic recipe can be cooked in minutes. Thyme is quite a strong herb, so you only need to add a small amount for the required flavour.

2 tbsp olive oil
1 onion, finely chopped
1 clove of garlic, crushed
400 g (14 oz) canned plum tomatoes, chopped (reserve the juice)
5 tbsp dry white wine
¼ tsp fresh thyme, chopped
1 tsp fresh basil, chopped
1 bay leaf
1 tbsp fresh parsley, chopped
Salt and freshly ground black pepper
1 tbsp cornflour
675 g (1½ lb) prawns, shelled

1 Combine the olive oil, onion and garlic in a deep bowl and cook on HIGH for 5 minutes, stirring frequently.

2 Add the chopped tomatoes, wine, herbs, salt and pepper and stir together well. Heat for 2 minutes on HIGH.

3 Mix the reserved tomato juice with the cornflour and add to the sauce. Cook on HIGH for 3 minutes and stir well until completely blended.

4 Add the prawns to the sauce and cook on HIGH for 2-4 minutes or until they are tender and the sauce has thickened. Remove the bay leaf before serving on a bed of rice or pasta.

Bunches of dried thyme flowers can be hung in linen cupboards to ward off insects. Tie a ribbon around the bottom of the stalks and hang them upside-down. Alternatively, remove the flowers from the stalks and place them in a small fabric sachet.

Bergamot

Bergamot (Monarda didyma) is a fragrant herb with bright red flowers and pale green, red-tinged leaves. Its attractive appearance has led to its popularity as a garden plant. It prefers a rich, moist soil and partial shade and needs to be kept well watered, especially in hot weather. Bergamot can grow to a height of 45-100 cm (18-36 in). Its distinctive scarlet flowers bloom in late summer.

One of bergamot's common names is bee balm because bees are attracted by its scent and nectar. The plant is native to North America, where it was first discovered by early settlers and was used by Oswego Indians to make tea, hence its other common name of Oswego tea.

Its chopped leaves and flowers can be used to add colour and an orangey flavour to green salads, jellies, fruit cups and fruit salads.

March

22

Bergamot can act as a mild sedative when added to hot milk.

23

24

25

26

27

At the time of the Boston Tea Party of 1773, settlers preferred to drink tea made from bergamot rather than that imported from Britain.

28

Grape and Bergamot Jellies

Serves 4

These individual jellies only take a few minutes to cook in the microwave. They make a refreshing end to a meal. Decorate them with rosettes of cream, if desired.

120 g (4 oz) green grapes
430 ml (¾ pint) unsweetened white grape juice
30 g (2 tbsp) sugar
15 g (1 tbsp) powdered gelatine
140 ml (¼ pint) water
4 sprigs of bergamot

1 If the grapes are not seedless, cut in half and remove the pips. Skin the grapes if desired.

2 Put the grape juice, sugar and bergamot in a large bowl and cook on HIGH for 2-4 minutes until the sugar has dissolved, stirring once. Allow to cool slightly, then remove the bergamot.

3 Mix the gelatine with 60 ml (4 tbsp) of the water. Cook on HIGH for 30 seconds, stir and cook for a further 30 seconds if necessary to dissolve the gelatine. Stir in the grape juice and add the remaining water.

4 Divide the grapes between the four glasses and pour in the jelly. Chill in the refrigerator until set.

Courgettes in Tomato and Bergamot Sauce

Serves 4

This colourful dish makes an ideal accompaniment to grilled chicken or steak. If you do not wish to cook it in a microwave, fry everything gently in a frying pan and simply increase the cooking time until the vegetables are tender and the bacon is well cooked.

4 rashers of rindless streaky bacon, chopped
1 large onion, peeled and finely chopped
1 clove of garlic, peeled and crushed
700 g (1½ lb) courgettes, sliced diagonally
400 g (14 oz) can tomatoes, chopped
30 ml (2 tbsp) bergamot, finely chopped
Salt and freshly ground black pepper

1 Place the bacon in a small bowl and cook uncovered on HIGH for 1-2 minutes until crisp.

2 Stir in the onion and garlic and cook on HIGH for 2 minutes.

3 Add the remaining ingredients and mix well. Cover and cook on HIGH for 10-15 minutes until the vegetables are tender.

Yarrow

Yarrow (Achillea millefolium) is a hardy perennial which will grow almost anywhere. It has dark green feathery leaves and clusters of white or pale lilac flowers which bloom throughout the summer. It grows in small bushes, reaching a height of 60 cm (2 ft). The leaves and flowers both give off a pleasant fragrance when crushed.

Yarrow is used for cosmetic and medicinal, rather than culinary purposes. In ancient times, it was said to have been used by Achilles to heal the bleeding wounds of his army, leading to it being known as Soldier's Woundwort, Staunchweed and Herbe Militaris. More recently, it was used to help the formation of scar tissue.

Yarrow was also once used in witchcraft, resulting in its other country names of Devil's Plaything, Devil's Nettle and Bad Man's Plaything.

A pinch of yarrow, wrapped up in a piece of flannel and placed under the pillow at bedtime, was supposed to bring a vision of a future husband or wife.

March

29

In Sweden yarrow is known as Field Hop and has been used to brew an intoxicating beer.

30

31

Yarrow is supposed to prevent baldness if the head is washed in an infusion of it.

Pressed Herb Cards

Everyone appreciates the time and effort that goes into a home-made present. These delightful cards are easy to make and could also be framed by the recipient. The secrets of success are to press the flowers carefully and to use textured, hand-made papers for the background. As well as using flowers, also press a variety of herb leaves as these either make good backgrounds or are attractive enough in their own right to be used.

You will need

Fresh herb flowers and leaves
White blotting paper
Flower press
Hand-made paper
Rubber-based glue
Card

1 Gather a good selection of fresh herb flowers and leaves. Place them in single layers between sheets of clean, white blotting paper and press tightly in a flower press for several weeks. The blotting paper will absorb any moisture as the herbs gradually dry. Use white blotting paper as the dye can 'bleed' from coloured papers. If you do not have a flower press, place the herbs and blotting paper between the pages of a heavy book and weight down.

2 When the herbs have dried, carefully remove the sheets of blotting paper. The herbs will now be very fragile so take care not to tear the delicate petals. You may find it easier to use a pair of tweezers or forceps to position the herbs.

3 Arrange the herbs in your chosen design on a rectangle of hand-made paper. Carefully glue in position using a rubber-based glue. If you wish, you can write a greeting on the front using an ink pen.

4 Stick the decorated rectangle onto a slightly larger folded card. If you are sending these cards through the post, use fairly thick envelopes to make sure the cards are not damaged in transit.

Yarrow Face Cleanser

Yarrow leaves and flowers make a good herb cleanser suitable for oily skins. Make an infusion of yarrow by placing 3 level tablespoons of leaves and flowers in a bowl and pouring over 150 ml (¼ pint) boiling water. Leave the infusion to cool, then strain and bottle in clean containers. This cleanser will keep in the refrigerator for a couple of days.

April

Chervil

Chervil (Anthriscus cerefolium) is one of the easiest herbs to grow. It is a fern-like plant, resembling parsley, and grows to a height of about 45 cm (18 in). Like parsley, there are both flat and curly-leaved varieties available. Chervil has pale green leaves and small white flowers, and prefers a well drained, partially shady site.

Its aniseed taste is fairly subtle, so use generous quantities when cooking with it and add to dishes towards the end of the cooking time. Widely used in French cuisine, its flavour goes well with fish, chicken and salad dishes. Chervil is combined with parsley, tarragon and thyme for the classic fines herbes mix used in French cooking. These are very finely chopped herbs often used to flavour omelettes and other egg dishes and used as a garnish.

Chervil is traditionally one of the Lenten herbs, symbolic of new life and rebirth and thought to have blood-cleansing properties. It was used in great quantities during Lent, both in cooking and as a skin cleanser.

If you like the taste of hot, peppery radishes, try growing a few chervil plants in the vegetable plot alongside the radishes. The chervil will help keep away harmful bugs and insects and the radishes growing closest to the herbs will have a slightly hotter flavour.

April

1

2

Chervil is often served on Holy Thursday as it represents new life and rebirth.

3

4

Combined with parsley, tarragon and thyme, chervil is one of the herbs used in the classic *fines herbes* mix used in French cooking.

5

6

7

Truite Meunière aux Herbes

Serves 4

According to the French story, the miller (meunier) used to catch trout from the mill stream and his wife used the flour from the mill to dredge them. Don't coat the fish in flour too soon before cooking or they will become soggy. Serve the fish with new potatoes and a green vegetable.

4 even-sized trout, cleaned and trimmed
Flour
Salt and freshly ground black pepper
100 g (4 oz) butter
2 tbsp chopped fresh herbs, such as chervil, parsley, tarragon, thyme or marjoram
Lemon wedges, to garnish

1 Trim the trout tails to make them more pointed. Rinse the trout well.

2 Dredge the fish with flour and shake off the excess. Season with salt and pepper. Heat half the butter in a large frying pan and, when foaming, add the trout. It may be necessary to cook the trout in two batches to avoid overcrowding the pan.

3 Cook the fish over a fairly high heat, browning both sides evenly. The fish should take 5-8 minutes per side to cook, depending on size. The dorsal fin will pull out easily when the fish is cooked. Remove the trout to a serving dish and keep warm.

4 Wipe out the pan and add the remaining butter. Cook over a moderate heat until beginning to brown, then add the lemon juice and herbs. When the lemon juice is added, the butter will bubble and sizzle. Pour over the fish immediately and garnish with lemon wedges.

Cheese and Chervil Spread

For quick canapés, mix together 100 g (4 oz) cream cheese, 2 tbsp of sour cream or natural yoghurt and 3 tbsp of chopped chervil and spread on vegetable sticks. Add extra sour cream or yoghurt to make a runnier dip to accompany crudités.

Curly-leaf Parsley

Parsley (Petroselium crispum) is one of the most popular herbs available. There are two varieties – the curly-leaved and the flat-leaved. The curly variety is most often used for garnishing dishes. Its leaves are divided into small segments with the edges tightly curled. The plant varies in height from dwarf varieties which are suitable for growing on kitchen windowsills and in window boxes to varieties which can reach 60 cm (2 ft) in height. It prefers a sunny position and rich, moist soil.

Parsley is said to grow best when the woman of the house wears the trousers. This could be linked to the old country beliefs that a parsley bed was where babies were discovered, and that unmarried pregnant girls could solve their predicament by chewing parsley three times a day for a period of three weeks. Parsley has also been associated with death since the ancient Greeks dedicated it to funeral rites. It was their custom to scatter it on graves, weave it into crowns for victors in sporting games and feed it to chariot horses before races.

An old French remedy for swellings was to apply a poultice of pounded parsley and snails.

April

8

9

Chew parsley leaves to sweeten the breath.

10

11

12

13

If parsley is scattered in fishponds, it is said to heal sick fish.

14

Cheese and Herb Scones

Makes 10

These tasty scones can be made with parsley, chives or marjoram, or a mixture of all three. Serve them warm, sliced and spread with butter for a perfect afternoon tea-time treat. They are best eaten on the day of baking.

100 g (4 oz) self-raising white flour
2 tsp baking powder
100 g (4 oz) plain wholemeal flour
pinch of salt
½ tsp paprika
50 g (2 oz) margarine
75 g (3 oz) cheese, finely grated
4 tsp chopped fresh herbs
8 tbsp milk
milk, to glaze

1 Pre-heat the oven to 220°C/425°F/gas mark 7. Sieve the self-raising flour and baking powder and place in a large bowl with the wholemeal flour. Add salt and paprika and rub in the margarine.

2 Add the cheese, herbs and milk and mix to form a soft dough. Place on a floured board and knead gently.

3 Roll out the dough to a thickness of 1 cm (½ in) and cut out the scones using a 5 cm (2 in) pastry cutter. Place on a greased baking tray and brush the top with milk. Bake in the oven for 10-15 minutes. Cool on a wire rack.

Parsley Mayonnaise

This recipe is a variation on traditional mayonnaise. It can be served with fish or with all types of salad dishes. Mayonnaise is simple to make with a blender or food processor.

1 tsp freshly made English mustard
1 egg
1 egg yolk
3 tbsp lemon juice
300 ml (10 fl oz) sunflower or grapeseed oil
Salt and freshly ground black pepper
1 tbsp chopped fresh parsley

1 Put the mustard, egg and egg yolk in the blender or food processor and blend for 15 seconds. Leave the machine running and very slowly add the oil, a drop at a time at first and then slightly faster. Continue to process until the mayonnaise is thick and creamy.

2 Add the lemon juice and seasoning and process for a few seconds. Stir in the chopped parsley. Serve immediately or store for up to 2 weeks in a screw-top jar in the refrigerator.

Parsley Sauce

Serves 4

Parsley sauce is one of the classic accompaniments for fish. Serve with plain grilled or poached fish.

2 tbsp butter
4 tbsp plain white flour
300 ml (10 fl oz) milk
Salt and freshly ground black pepper
1 tbsp chopped fresh parsley

1 Melt the butter in a saucepan and stir in the flour. Cook over a gentle heat for 2 minutes, stirring.

2 Remove from the heat and blend in a little of the milk. Add the rest of the milk, stirring all the time to make sure there are no lumps. Season with salt and pepper.

3 Return to the heat and bring to the boil, stirring. Reduce the heat and simmer gently for 5 minutes, stirring. Add the parsley, stir well and serve immediately.

Ginger Mint

Ginger mint (Mentha gentilis) comes from a cross between corn mint and spearmint, and has the strong smell of the latter. It is a perennial herb, growing to a height of 30-60 cm (1-2 ft) and producing smallish light green leaves. In the variegated form bright yellow stripes run through the leaves.

Ginger mint produces small, pale purple flowers which bloom along the main stem, rather than at the end of the stalk like other mints. It is also known as slender mint and Scotch mint and, when dried, its scented leaves are a useful addition to pot pourris. Like all mints, ginger mint can get out of control so try growing it in either in a pot or a container sunk into the ground to prevent the roots spreading too far.

April

15

16

Mice dislike the smell of either fresh or dried mint, so they will not touch any food where mint is scattered.

17

18

In the fourteenth century mint was used for whitening the teeth.

19

20

21

Herb Pot Pourris

Make your own pot pourris in the colours and scents of your choice. There are so many flowering herbs and scented leaves available that you can easily concoct your own recipes.

1 Gather the flowers and foliage when they are quite dry. Lay them out on trays covered in kitchen paper (to absorb moisture) and place in a warm room or airing cupboard. Leave them to dry thoroughly.

2 When dry, mix together the herbs and flowers in different colour and scent combinations.

3 To help prolong the fragrance of the herbs, mix in a fixative which will absorb the herbs' oils. Many fixatives themselves are scented and so add to the overall perfume of the pot pourri. Fixatives include cinnamon powder, orris root powder, nutmeg, cloves, vanilla pods and the seeds of coriander, cumin and angelica. Mix the fixative with a couple of drops of essential oil in a large bowl before adding the dried herbs.

The green raffia basket contains a sweetly scented pot pourri of rose petals, scented geranium leaves and eau de cologne mint. The gold basket displays a pot pourri with a much sharper scent, including apple mint, ginger mint, lemon verbena and lemon thyme, plus marigolds to add a splash of colour.

Mint Juleps

Mint juleps are refreshing bourbon-based cocktails served over crushed ice and mint. The drink is originally from the American South and many 'official' recipes exist. The drink became so popular in America in the mid-nineteenth century that temperance campaigners in the state of Virginia demanded that all mint beds be destroyed!

For each serving:
3 sprigs of fresh mint
½ tsp caster sugar
1 tbsp soda water
Crushed ice cubes
1 measure of bourbon
Sprig of mint, to decorate

Crush the mint in a tumbler with the sugar and rub it around the inside of the glass. Discard the mint. Add the soda water and stir until the sugar dissolves. Add the crushed ice and pour over the bourbon, but do not stir. Decorate with a sprig of mint.

Lemon Thyme

Lemon thyme (Thymus citriodorus) is a sweetly scented, evergreen herb and a cultivated form of wild thyme. It is a popular culinary herb due to its mild citrus flavour and is often used in stuffings, with chicken dishes or added to fruit salads and jellies.

Bees are attracted to lemon thyme and it gives honey a good flavour. It grows to a height of 20-30 cm (8-12 in) and prefers a dry, well drained soil. It produces dark pink flowers which bloom in late summer and it is the small green leaves that smell strongly of lemon. It is not as hardy as other thymes so may need protecting in winter with a layer of leaf mould or straw. This is a good variety for growing in containers. The dried, scented leaves make a useful, fragrant addition to pot pourri or scented sachets.

April

22

23

24

25

A tisane made from thyme is said to help speed recovery from a hangover.

26

27

28

Lemons Pickled with Rosemary and Bay

These lemon slices are perfect to accompany cold or roast meats and the oil can be used in salad dressings and marinades.

900 g (2 lb) lemons
Salt
Bay leaves
Rosemary sprigs
600 ml (1 pint) olive oil, or a mixture of olive oil and vegetable oil

1 Slice the lemons thinly and discard any pips. Layer the slices in a colander with plenty of salt. Sit the colander on a plate to catch any drips, cover with a clean tea towel and leave in a cool place for 24 hours.

2 Rinse the lemon slices and dry on kitchen paper. Place in a preserving jar with the herbs.

3 Pour in the oil, making sure the lemon slices are completely covered to prevent them turning mouldy. Seal the jar and store in the refrigerator for a month to let the flavour develop.

Salade de Légumes

Serves 6

This salad takes only minutes to prepare in the microwave, yet it is special enough for a dinner party. Either serve it as a starter or add tuna fish for a slightly more substantial main course.

270-300 g (9-10 oz) canned artichoke hearts
1 red onion, peeled and chopped
1 clove of garlic, chopped
1 green pepper, seeded and chopped
1 tsp chopped fresh thyme
1 tsp chopped fresh basil
2 tsp chopped fresh parsley
450 g (1 lb) canned haricot beans, white kidney beans or butter beans, rinsed and drained
4 tomatoes, peeled, seeded and chopped

Dressing

3 tbsp olive oil
2 tbsp white wine vinegar
½ tsp Dijon mustard
Pinch of salt and freshly ground black pepper
Radicchio and curly endive, to garnish

1 Stir all the ingredients, except the dressing and the garnish, together in a large bowl and cook on HIGH for 2 minutes to warm through.

2 Mix together the ingredients for the dressing, pour over the salad ingredients and toss to coat thoroughly.

3 Arrange the radicchio and endive on serving plates and spoon on the salad. Pour over any excess dressing. Serve warm.

White Lavender

White lavender is less common than the usual purple variety as it is not as resistant to disease, bad weather conditions or poor soil. However, there are five varieties available: the tiny Lavandula angustifolia 'Nana Alba' and the medium-sized 'Alba'; a white form of Lavandula stoechas which grows well in a container; the greenish-white Lavandula viridis, one of the taller growing species; and finally, the hardier Lavandula x intermedia 'Alba'.

There is also a pale pink variety available, Lavandula angustifolia 'Rosea', although some purple plants do produce the odd pink flower here and there. These paler lavenders seem to have a stronger scent than the darker purple varieties.

April

29

Bees prefer lavender to any other flower so you often find lavender bushes covered with bees searching for nectar.

30

31

Napoleon Bonaparte is rumoured to have been particularly fond of lavender water.

Lavender and Rose Wreath

Hang this wreath of dried lavender and roses in a warm place and its sweet fragrance will scent the room. When the smell begins to fade, revive it by sprinkling a few drops of lavender oil on the wreath. Undecorated wreaths are available in various shapes and sizes from craft shops and good florists.

You will need:

Dried lavender
Dried roses
Straw wreath
Florists' wire
Sharp scissors
Ribbon, for hanging

1 Group the lavender into small bunches of about eight stems. Wrap a length of florists' wire tightly around the stems, near the flower heads, leaving long ends of wire for attaching the bunch to the wreath. Cut off and discard the ends of the stalks.

2 Attach the bunches of lavender to the wreath by wrapping the wire around the wreath and twisting it tightly on the back of the wreath. Work in one direction, laying the flower heads over the stalks of the previous bunch to hide them.

3 When you have finished attaching the lavender, add the dried roses. Cut their stems to about 5 cm (2 in) in length and slip them in between the lavender bunches to fill in any gaps. The roses should not need extra wire attached to them.

4 Attach a length of coordinating ribbon to the back of the wreath for hanging.

Lavender Bottles

These old fashioned bottles are made from bunches of fresh lavender and are used to scent clothes or linen.

1 Take a bunch of fresh lavender and tie the stems together tightly with string or ribbon just below the flower heads.

2 Bend the stems back so the flowers are enclosed within a 'framework' of stems.

3 Tie the stems together with either string or ribbon, attaching a loop so they can be hung inside a wardrobe. The bottles will gradually dry out and stay in shape.

May

Apple Mint

Apple mint (Mentha rotundifolia, M. suaveolens) has less invasive growing habits than other varieties of mint and will not take over the whole garden. It has a pleasant, fruity taste and is sweeter than other mints. Also known as round-leaved mint, it has wrinkled, round leaves which have an apple scent and can grow to a height of 60 cm (2 ft). It grows best in rich, moist soil and partial shade and produces lilac and cream flowers in late summer. Native to southern and western Europe, it is quite a hardy plant and is resistant to disease. It is used mainly for culinary purposes and its milder taste makes it ideal for use in fruit salads and fruit cups and punches.

Dried apple mint leaves retain their scent and make excellent pot pourri.

May

1

In ancient Greece it was the custom to perfume every part of the body with a different scent; mint was used on the arms.

2

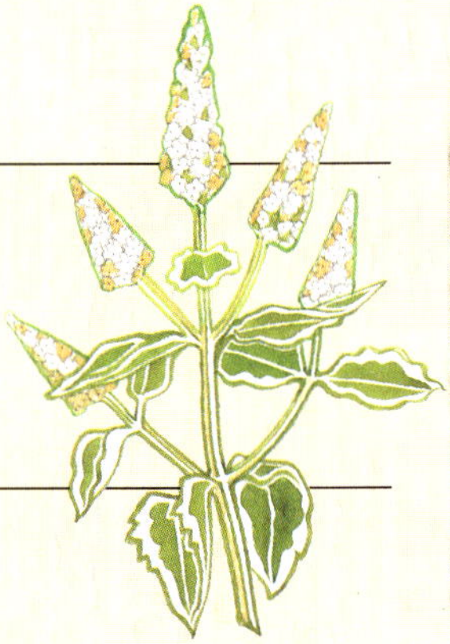

3

4

5

Mint leaves are said to relieve the pain caused by bee and wasp stings.

6

7

Prawns in Melon

Serves 4

This refreshing dish can be served as a light lunch accompanied by new potatoes and a mixed green salad. Alternatively, it will serve 8 people as a starter.

2 small melons
4 medium tomatoes
1 small cucumber
1 orange
Juice of half a lemon
4 tbsp vegetable oil
3 tbsp double cream
2 tbsp chopped fresh mint
Pinch of sugar
Salt and freshly ground black pepper
1 tsp chopped fresh lemon thyme
225 g (8 oz) peeled prawns
90 g (3 oz) toasted flaked almonds
Mint sprigs, to garnish

1 Cut the melons in half across the middle, remove and discard the seeds and scoop out the flesh with a melon baller or spoon. Leave a 5 mm (¼ in) border of fruit inside each shell.

2 Cut the melon flesh into 1 cm (½ in) cubes or leave in balls. Peel the tomatoes and remove the seeds. Cut the flesh into strips. Peel the cucumber, cut in half lengthways and then into 1 cm (½ in) cubes. Peel and segment the orange.

3 In a large bowl mix together the lemon juice, oil and double cream. Stir in the mint, sugar, salt and pepper and thyme. Add the prawns, fruit and vegetables and mix thoroughly to coat evenly with the dressing.

4 Pile equal quantities of the fruit and prawn mixture in the four melon shells and chill well. Serve garnished with mint sprigs and almonds.

Mint Foot Bath

Refresh tired and aching feet by soaking them in a soothing mint foot bath. Make an infusion of 1 tablespoon of mint and 2.25 litres (4 pints) boiling water. Leave the water to cool slightly and infuse for 15 minutes, then strain and immerse your feet in the scented warm water for 15 minutes.

Mint Sauce

This is the classic sauce to serve with roast lamb. Make 1 hour before serving to allow time for the flavour to develop.

Small bunch of mint
10 ml (2 tsp) sugar
15 ml (1 tbsp) boiling water
15-30 ml (1-2 tbsp) vinegar

Place the mint and sugar on a board and chop finely. Put in a sauceboat and add the boiling water. Stir until the sugar has dissolved. Stir in vinegar to taste.

Basil

Basil (Ocimum basilicum) has been cultivated for over two thousand years and probably originated in India, although it is seldom used in Indian cooking. It is one of the few herbs that cannot be dried successfully so always use fresh leaves. Young leaves are the sweetest so it is best to sow plenty of seeds to ensure a constant crop. It will thrive in a sunny position and light, rich soil, but do not be tempted to over-water. Growing to a height of 30-60 cm (1-2 ft), it has large, shiny leaves and small white flowers that bloom in clusters. Remove the flowers to encourage more leaf growth.

It is susceptible to frost damage, so grow basil in a pot that can be moved indoors during colder weather. Tear the leaves rather than chop them to preserve their flavour and add to hot dishes just before the end of the cooking time. Basil is widely used in Mediterranean cooking and it is the perfect partner for eggs and tomatoes. Although mainly used in cooking, basil can be dried and used as snuff to cure nervous headaches.

Basil is one of the herbs symbolising love. At one time young girls would place a pot of basil on their windowsill to show that suitors would be welcomed.

May

8

9

In Tudor times, farmers' wives traditionally gave small pots of basil as parting gifts to visitors.

10

11

12

13

In Moldavia, the custom is that a young man will love any girl from whom he accepts a sprig of basil.

14

Pesto Sauce

This is the classic Italian sauce to serve with pasta. Traditionally it should only be made when the basil is in flower. Although the basil can be pounded in a pestle and mortar, it is far quicker to use a food processor.

Medium bunch of fresh basil
60-90 ml (4-6 tbsp) olive oil
2 garlic cloves, skinned and crushed
25 g (1 oz) pine nuts
25 g (1 oz) fresh Parmesan cheese, grated

1 Mix all the ingredients, apart from the Parmesan, in a blender or food processor and mix until smooth.

2 Stir in the Parmesan and add more oil if a thinner consistency is required. Serve with fresh pasta.

Tomato and Orange Salad

Serves 4

Tomatoes, mozzarella cheese and basil are a common salad combination as their flavours go together so well. The addition of oranges makes this recipe just a little bit different. Shred the basil leaves just before serving as they tend to turn black if cut and left to stand.

4 large beef tomatoes
4 small oranges
225 g (8 oz) mozzarella cheese
8 fresh basil leaves
60 ml (4 tbsp) olive oil
15 ml (1 tbsp) white wine vinegar
Salt and freshly ground black pepper

1 Remove the cores from the tomatoes and slice horizontally into rounds about 5 mm (¼ in) thick.

2 Cut a slice from the top and bottom of each orange and, using a serrated fruit knife, remove the peel in thin strips and cut off all the white pith. Slice the oranges into 5 mm (¼ in) thick rounds and remove any pips. Slice the mozzarella into slices of the same thickness.

3 Arrange the tomatoes, oranges and mozzarella in overlapping circles, alternating each ingredient. Shred the basil and sprinkle over the salad.

4 Mix the remaining ingredients together and spoon over the salad. Chill briefly before serving.

Garlic Chives

Garlic chives (Allium sativum) are very similar to normal chives but, as their name suggests, have a distinct garlic flavour. They are part of the same botanical family as garlic, onions, leeks and shallots and can be added to salads and other uncooked dishes that benefit from a garlicky taste. Unlike other chives, they do not spread in the garden. The slender green stalks are flatter than those of ordinary chives and the bulbous flowers are paler in colour.

Garlic chives grow to a height of 15-25 cm (6-10 in) and will grow in ordinary garden soil. They can also be grown indoors in pots and are suitable for window boxes.

May

15

Chives grow in thick clumps and can be used as edging plants.

16

17

18

Chives are easy to freeze – simply place cut stalks in polythene bags and place in the freezer.

19

20

21

Trout with Chive Sauce

Serves 4

This trout recipe is perfect for a dinner party. Serve with new potatoes and a green vegetable such as mangetout.

4 even-sized rainbow trout, gutted and fins trimmed
Flour mixed with salt and pepper for dredging
60 ml (4 tbsp) butter, melted
30 ml (2 tbsp) white wine
280 ml (½ pint) double cream
1 small bunch of chives, chopped
Salt and freshly ground black pepper

1 Dredge the trout with the seasoned flour and place on a lightly greased baking sheet. Spoon the melted butter over the fish.

2 Bake in a 400° F/200° C/gas mark 6 oven for about 10 minutes, basting frequently with butter, until the skin is crisp. Check the fish on the underside close to the bone. If it is not cooked through, lower the temperature to 325° F/170°C/gas mark 3 and cook for a further 5 minutes.

3 Pour the wine into a small saucepan and bring to the boil. Boil to reduce by half. Pour in the cream and bring back to the boil and boil until the cream thickens slightly. Stir in the chopped chives, saving some for a garnish.

4 When the fish are browned, place in a serving dish, pour over some of the sauce and garnish with chives. Serve the rest of the sauce separately.

Companion Planting

Companion planting is the name given to the gardening theory that some plants will flourish when planted near particular species and will do badly in the presence of others. This is especially true of herbs as the following list shows. With the exception of fennel, most herbs planted in or near vegetable beds will have a beneficial effect. Try planting herbs at the corners of beds to ward off flies and various insects and to attract bees.

Basil – does not grow well near rue, but will benefit most vegetables.
Borage – will encourage strawberries, cucumbers and tomatoes.
Chamomile – helps wheat, onions and cabbage.
Chervil – grows well with radishes (the radishes growing closest to the chervil will have a hotter taste).
Chives – improve the health of apple trees and increase the size of carrots, but will not help beans.
Coriander – slows down the formation of fennel seed.
Dill – encourages the growth of cabbages and corn, but not carrots.
Fennel – has a bad effect on tomatoes, turnips and dwarf beans, but will improve lettuce and leeks.
Horseradish – grows well with potatoes and makes them more resistant to disease.
Hyssop – attracts cabbage butterfly away from cabbages and will increase the growth of grapes if planted near a grapevine, but has a detrimental effect on radishes.
Marigold – improves the growth of tomatoes and deters flies.
Nasturtium – keeps broccoli and apple trees free from aphids; also helps radishes.
Parsley – benefits roses and tomatoes.
Peppermint – protects cabbages from cabbage butterfly.
Rosemary – deters carrot fly; rosemary and sage benefit each other.
Sage – grows well with rosemary, but does not encourage the growth of cucumbers.
Southernwood – helps fruit trees.
Summer savory – benefits green beans and onions.
Tansy – keeps flies away from peach trees.
Thyme – discourages cabbage root fly.
Valerian – helps most vegetables.
Winter savory – slows down the germination of some seeds.
Yarrow – helps most vegetables.

Spearmint

Spearmint (Mentha spicata) is one of the best known and most widely cultivated mints. It is one of the oldest culinary herbs and is thought to be a cross of horse-mint and round-leaved mint. It grows to a height of 45 cm (18 in) and is best grown in a container to prevent it running wild and taking over the whole garden. A native of the Mediterranean region, this mint was introduced to America by the Pilgrim Fathers. It prefers a rich, moist soil and should be cut back to encourage new growth from the roots.

Spearmint produces long spikes of lilac flowers in summer. This mint goes under a number of different names, including garden mint, mackerel mint, our lady's mint, sage of Bethlehem, fish mint and lamb mint. Its generic name, Mentha, comes from ancient Greek mythology – Mentha was a nymph metamorphosed into the plant we now call mint.

May

22

23

24

The application of a strong decoction of spearmint is reputed to heal chapped hands.

25

26

27

Woe unto you, for ye pay a tithe of mint and anise and cumin.

Matthew 23

28

Linen Sachets

These fabric envelopes are filled with a mixture of wadding and dried moth-repellant herbs, including southernwood, mint, tansy and thyme. Add dried rose petals or lavender for a floral perfume, or dried crushed cloves for a spicier scent. Place these sachets in a linen chest or cupboard to keep moths at bay.

You will need:

Pretty cotton or linen handkerchiefs
Matching thread
Scraps of wadding
Beads, to decorate (optional)
Dried herb mixture (as above)

1 Iron the handkerchiefs and press the four corners into the centre, overlapping the edges slightly, to form an envelope. If the handkerchief has an embroidered corner, use this as the top flap.

2 Sew together the bottom and two side edges with a small running stitch. If you wish, decorate the top flap with pretty beads and sequins.

3 Fill the envelopes with the wadding and herb mixture. The top flap can be stitched down to secure the contents.

4 The larger sachet is made with a length of embroidered linen, such as a tray cloth. Fold the cloth into three and stitch the sides of the bottom and middle sections together to form an envelope. The embroidered top section folds over to enclose the wadding and herbs.

Herb Ice Cubes

Give your drinks a festive look by freezing herbs with water in ice cube trays. Nasturtium petals and leaves, borage flowers and mint leaves are all ideal and will add a splash of colour. Fill an ice cube tray half-full, add the herbs and freeze. Top up the ice cube tray and return to the freezer. If you are planning a party, it is easy to make large batches of these ice cubes in advance.

Fresh Herb Wreath

A wreath decorated with fresh herbs takes only minutes to make if you use a loosely woven cane wreath. Simply gather a selection of fresh herbs and thread their stalks into the wreath. There is no need to glue or wire them into position. Add a matching ribbon to hang the wreath. When the herbs die, replace them with another arrangement of green foliage. The herbs used here include thyme, various mints, rosemary and basil.

Nasturtiums

Nasturtiums (Tropaeolum majus) are among the prettiest of all herbs, with their cheerful trumpet-shaped red, yellow and orange flowers providing a brilliant splash of colour in summer months. The flowers are unscented but they are frequently visited by bees due to the large quantities of nectar they produce. The flowers are one of the most popular edible blooms and are often used in salads and as garnishes. Chopped blossoms can be added to butters and cream cheese. The aromatic, round, flat leaves have a peppery taste, similar to that of watercress.

These trailing or climbing annuals grow well in a sunny site with light, sandy soil. They are ideal plants for window boxes or containers as they bloom prolifically and they will keep away flies and other insects. There are various types available, including dwarf, trailing or climbing varieties and a hybrid with variegated green and cream leaves.

Nasturtiums originate from South America and were brought to Europe by the conquistadors in the sixteenth century.

May

29

The nasturtium plant is a good source of vitamin C and it was once eaten as a remedy for scurvy.

30

31

The word nasturtium is derived form the Latin 'nasus tortus' (meaning a convulsed nose) due to its pungent scent.

Floating Candles

A bowl of scented floating candles and nasturtiums makes an extremely elegant and unusual centrepiece for a dinner party. Buy the small floating candles in bright colours to match the nasturtiums.

Half-fill a decorative glass bowl with water and carefully float the flowers and candles on the surface. If you have some small nasturtium leaves, add these to the bowl as well. You should aim to cover the entire surface of the water. The candles will not burn for very long, so do not light them until your guests are ready to sit down and eat.

If nasturtiums are not available, use marigold or borage flowers or a variety of green herb leaves. Alternatively, place a small bowl by each place setting and decorate with a single candle and a few leaves. However, be sure to position them where guests will not catch their sleeves on the flame.

Pickled Nasturtiums

These make a very good substitute for capers and can be used in sauces or as a garnish for savoury dishes. The nasturtium pods can be gathered from midsummer.

For each pint of wine or cider vinegar you will need 25 g (1 oz) salt, 6 peppercorns and sufficient nasturtiums to fill a 600 ml (1 pint) storage jar. Gather the nasturtium pods on a dry day and wipe them clean with kitchen paper. Place them in a dry glass jar with the vinegar, salt and pepper. Seal the jar and store for several weeks before using.

Nasturtium vinegar can also be made by filled a wide-necked glass jar with white wine vinegar and nasturtium flowers. Leave the filled jar in a warm place (but out of direct sunlight) for several weeks until the vinegar has absorbed the colour of the nasturtiums. Strain the vinegar and use it to add extra flavour to salad dressings.

In French cookery nasturtium flowers and leaves are used in the same way as vine leaves, and are stuffed with sweet or savoury fillings.

June

Lovage

Lovage (Levisticum officinale) is a large perennial which can grow up to 2.5 m (8 ft) in height. It has large green leaves divided into segments and small greenish-yellow flowers which bloom from late summer. Lovage grows well in a moist soil and sunny position.

The leaves are similar to those of angelica and celery and have a strong, yeasty taste which should be used sparingly to add extra flavour to meat and vegetable dishes. The young leaves can be simmered in water until tender and served as a green vegetable. Fresh leaves can be added to green salads.

Lovage was widely used for medicinal purposes in the fourteenth century, mainly because of its pleasant aroma. Lovage is one of the few herbs without any myths or legends attached to it.

June

1

2

In Mediterranean cookery crushed lovage seeds are used to add flavour to breads, cakes and biscuits.

3

4

5

Crushed lovage leaves can be rubbed onto meat before cooking to improve the flavour.

6

7

Trout with Lovage and Yogurt Sauce

Serves 4

This dish takes only 10 minutes to prepare and less than 20 minutes to cook in the microwave, yet it is special enough to serve to dinner guests.

15 ml (½ oz) butter
60 g (2 oz) flaked almonds
5 ml (1 tsp) celery seeds
30 ml (2 tbsp) chopped fresh lovage
4 medium trout, cleaned
Salt and freshly ground black pepper
15 ml (1 tbsp) cornflour
140 ml (¼ pint) natural yogurt

1 Put the butter, almonds and celery seeds into a shallow dish and cook, uncovered, on HIGH for 4-8 minutes, stirring frequently, until the almonds begin to brown. Set aside.

2 Divide half the chopped lovage between the four trout, place inside each fish and season with salt and pepper.

3 Arrange the fish head to tail in a shallow dish and cook on HIGH for 6-8 minutes until the fish is cooked, repositioning halfway through cooking. Set aside and keep warm.

4 Mix the cornflour with a little of the yogurt in a small bowl and then add the remaining yogurt. Cook on HIGH for 2-4 minutes, whisking frequently until thickened. Stir in the remaining lovage.

5 Serve the trout with the sauce and garnish with the browned almonds.

Tansy

Tansy (*Tanecetum vulgare*) is a hardy perennial with aromatic green leaves and clusters of yellow flowers, which have given it its common name of 'buttons'. It has a hot, bitter, though not unpleasant, taste. It is one of the taller herbs, reaching a height of 100-125 cm (3-4 ft). It will thrive in most types of soil and grows wild in many places. If growing wild, tansy will be eaten by cows and sheep, but horses and goats will not touch it.

Although an essential ingredient in many recipes dating from Elizabethan times, tansy is no longer widely used in cooking and is now grown mainly for decorative purposes. Its name is derived from the Greek for 'immortal', probably because its flowers last for so long.

Tansy has an old connection with Easter, when tansy cakes were made from the young leaves and were eaten to sweeten body odours resulting from the limited food eaten during Lent.

'In their blooming season, he liked a few marigold heads in his mutton broth, and tansy flowers in his rice pudding.'

Still Glides The Stream
Flora Thompson

June

8

9

10

11

Tansy was one of the herbs used for strewing in the sixteenth century.

12

13

14

In Finland tansy is used to produce green dye.

Linen Drawer Sachets

These slender sachets are filled with an aromatic mix of moth-repellant herbs, including tansy, southernwood and lavender to add a pleasing fragrance. You can either use embroidered cloth, as shown here, or a pretty floral cotton fabric.

You will need:

Rectangle of fabric 15 x 25 cm (6 x 10 in)
Piece of wadding 7.5 x 25 cm (3 x 10 in)
Dried herbs

1 Fold the fabric in half lengthways, right sides facing and pin wadding underneath, as shown.

2 Sew along the two short edges and trim back any excess wadding.

3 Turn right sides out and fill the sachet with herbs, making sure they are evenly distributed. Hand-stitch the third seam to finish.

Rhubarb Tansy

Serves 4

Since Elizabethan times tansy has been associated with rhubarb dishes.

450 g (1 lb) rhubarb, trimmed and cut into 2.5 cm (1 in) lengths
Pinch of ground ginger
60 ml (4 tbsp) water
2 eggs, separated
2 tsp chopped tansy
Juice and zest of 1 lemon
90 g (3 oz) sugar
140 ml (¼ pint) double cream

1 Put the rhubarb in a large bowl with the ginger and water. Cover and cook on HIGH for 10-12 minutes, stirring twice, until the rhubarb is mushy.

2 Stir in the egg yolks, tansy, lemon juice and zest. Purée in a food processor or blender.

3 Whisk the egg whites to form soft peaks, then whisk in the sugar, half at a time.

4 Whip the cream to form soft peaks and fold into the rhubarb mixture. Fold in the egg whites and spoon the mixture into glasses. Chill thoroughly before serving with crisp biscuits.

Tansy is one of the bitter herbs eaten at the Jewish Passover.

Summer Savory

Summer savory (Satureia hortensis) is a small herb growing to a height of 15-30 cm (6-12 in). It produces small, leafy bushes of small, narrow green leaves with delicate blue and white flowers. Originally from Mediterranean regions, summer savory grows best in a light, rich soil with plenty of sun. It has an aromatic, spicy flavour and is a good partner for fish, meat and eggs as well as vegetables such as beans and peas. It was a popular herb with the ancient Greeks and Romans who used it extensively in sauces for meat and fish and to flavour vinegars. Although mainly a culinary herb, summer savory was added to medicines simply for its fragrance and it was also said to be useful in treating colic.

June

15

16

17

18

Winter and summer savory were introduced to America by English colonists.

19

20

21

Spiced Apples with Summer Savory

Serves 4

Serve this refreshing dessert either warm or cold with whipped cream. Use either dessert apples or apples that hold their shape when cooked.

675 g (1½ lb) apples
1 cinnamon stick
3 cloves
Sugar, to taste
2 tsp chopped summer savory
60 ml (4 tbsp) white wine
Whipped cream, to serve

1 Peel, core and thickly slice the apples. Put them in a heavy saucepan with the sugar, spices and enough water just to cover them. Cook slowly, covered, for about 10-15 minutes until the apples are soft and slightly translucent. Do not allow the apples to boil or they will break up.

2 When the apples are cooked, remove them from the pan to a serving dish. Discard the cinnamon and cloves.

3 Add the chopped savory and wine to the syrup and slowly bring to the boil, stirring occasionally. Boil the syrup for 2 minutes to thicken slightly. Pour the syrup over the apples and serve.

Savory has been used in cooking for thousands of years. In his writings, Virgil noted it as being one of the most fragrant herbs. It is believed that it was widely used to flavour foods before spices were brought from India and the East.

New Potatoes with Cheese and Summer Savory

Serves 4-5

The cheese used in this recipe is Bel Paese, an Italian soft cheese which has a mild, fruity flavour. It is often sold in individual portions.

900 g (2 lb) new potatoes, scrubbed but not peeled
180 g (6 oz) Bel Paese cheese
60-90 ml (4-6 tbsp) milk or single cream
Salt and freshly ground black pepper
Chopped summer savory

1 Cook the potatoes in salt water for 20 minutes or until tender. Drain and cut potatoes in half if they are large. Leave small potatoes whole.

2 Mix the cheese and milk or cream together. Add more milk or cream if the cheese is still too thick. Mix in salt and pepper and add the potatoes. Stir well to ensure the potatoes are well coated.

3 Sprinkle on the summer savory and serve immediately.

'Here's flowers for you;
Hot lavender, mints, savory,
marjoram'

The Winter's Tale
William Shakespeare

Eau de Cologne Mint

Eau de Cologne mint (Mentha citrata) is, as its name suggests, a fragrant mint with pale pink flowers. It is also known as lemon mint, orange mint, bergamot mint and lavender mint, depending on what its scent most reminds you of. It grows to a height of 50 cm (20 in) and spreads invasively, producing runners that grow both above and below the ground, so grow this mint in a pot if you wish to contain it. If grown in a sunny position, the mint will develop its characteristic scent and will be purplish in colour. The plant will be greener if grown in the shade.

This is an ideal mint to dry for pot pourris and for use in scented sachets as its scent is better than its flavour. However, it can be used to flavour vinegar.

June

22

23

24

'A little path of mintes full and fenill greene'

Chaucer

25

26

All mints possess fragrant oils which can be extracted by distillation.

27

28

Herb Posies

Small bunches of herbs fresh from the garden make delightful gifts. Gather together herbs in various shades of green with different types of foliage and arrange with a variety of herb flowers. Tie the bunches with ribbon in a coordinating colour. Small posies like these would make charming bridesmaids' bouquets at a country wedding.

Guava Mint Sorbet

Serves 4-6

When a light dessert is called for, a sorbet cannot be surpassed. The exotic taste of guava works well with mint. The sorbet will keep in the freezer for up to 3 months in a well-sealed, rigid container.

4 ripe guavas
180 g (6 oz) granulated sugar
280 ml (½ pint) water
2 tbsp chopped fresh mint
1 lime
1 egg white
Fresh mint leaves, to garnish

1 Combine the sugar and water in a heavy-based saucepan and bring slowly to the boil to dissolve the sugar. When the mixture is a clear syrup, boil rapidly for 30 seconds. Allow to cool to room temperature then chill in the refrigerator.

2 Cut the guavas in half and scoop out the pulp. Discard the peel and seeds and purée the fruit in a food processor until smooth. Add the mint and combine with the cold syrup. Add lime juice until the right balance of sweetness is reached.

3 Pour the mixture into a shallow container and freeze until slushy. Process again to break up the ice crystals and then freeze again until firm.

4 Whip the egg white until stiff but not dry. Process the sorbet again and, when smooth, add the egg white. Mix once or twice and then freeze again until firm.

5 Remove from the freezer 15 minutes before serving and keep in the refrigerator. Scoop out and garnish each serving with mint leaves.

Marigold

Marigold (Calendula officinalis) is a popular hardy annual grown from seed and its cheerful, brightly coloured orange, cream or yellow flowers are often seen in country gardens. It will thrive in a sunny position and prefers a moist, rich soil. It is also suitable for growing in window boxes and containers or inside conservatories. Dead-head the plants frequently to encourage new flowers.

Marigolds are said to bloom on the calends (the first day) of every month, hence their botanical name. The chopped flowers can be added during the cheese-making process to provide colour, or scattered over salads, rice and egg dishes. They can be used as an alternative to saffron or can be added to sweet dishes, such as custards or baked puddings.

A marigold flower, when rubbed on to the affected area, is said to provide relief from bee and wasp stings.

A seventeenth century recipe advises that 'a conserve made of marigold flowers and sugar, taken in the morning fasting, cureth the trembling of the heart'.

June

29

The marigold is said to bloom between 9 am and 3 pm. Shakespeare called it 'the marigold that goes to bed wi' the sun, and rises with him weeping'.

30

An infusion made from marigold leaves will soothe tired feet.

Mixed Herb Tea

Combine your favourite herbs into a mixed herb tea. This is also a good way to include herbs which would taste far too strong to make into a tisane on their own. Experiment with different combinations of herbs until you find a mixture that suits your tastebuds. Most herbal teas should be infused for 3-4 minutes and they can be sweetened with honey if necessary. This tea shown here includes mint, lavender, marigolds, rose petals and dried orange peel.

Pot Pourri Sachet

This delicately-scented sachet is ideal for hanging in your wardrobe to keep clothes smelling sweet. Simply loop the ribbon over the hook of a coat hanger. All you need are a few small pieces of fabric and wadding and some fragrant pot pourri. Choose a fabric to match the colours of the pot pourri – the yellow mix used here includes dried marigold petals, lemon verbena leaves, lemon balm and eau de cologne mint.

You will need:

Two squares of fabric, 12 x 12 cm (4¾ x 4¾ in)
18 cm (7 in) length of lace
One square of net, 12 x 12 cm (4¾ x 4¾ in)
15 cm (6 in) length of ribbon
Terylene wadding
Pot pourri

1 Cut the piece of net in half diagonally. (The spare net triangle can be used to make a second sachet.)

2 Pin the net on the right side of one of the fabric squares. Pin the lace diagonally across, ensuring that the edge of the lace overlaps approximately 5 mm (¼ in) of the net.

3 Stitch the lace and net to the fabric with two lines of stitching, one line close to each edge. Make sure the net is firmly sewn in.

4 Place the two fabric squares right sides together, with the net and lace sandwiched in between. Pin and sew along one of the net sides.

5 Fill the net pocket with pot pourri.

6 Fold the fabric squares right sides together again and carefully pin and sew along the second net edge (to close the pot pourri pocket) and along a third side.

7 Turn the sachet rights sides out and stuff the sachet with wadding. Sew along the remaining seam, stitching in the hanging ribbon at one corner.

July

French Sorrel

French sorrel (Rumex scutatus), also known as Buckler's sorrel, is a herb native to the mountainous regions of France, Italy, Switzerland, Germany and western Asia. It is a member of the dock family. It has small leaves, as broad as they are long, and grows as a tangled plant of leafy stems to a height of 45 cm (1½ft). This type of sorrel has a less acidic taste than other sorrels so is the variety most often used in cooking, especially French cuisine, where it is made into sorrel soup. It prefers growing in shady positions with good soil and produces greenish-pink flowers. This herb freezes well because it has soft leaves.

July

1

2

During the reign of Henry VII, wood sorrel was held in great esteem as a pot herb.

3

4

5

6

'Golden grain, bright fruits,
Sweet herbs which grow for all.'

Edward Arnold

7

Bouquet Garnis

Bouquet garnis are bunches of fresh, aromatic herbs which are used to add flavour to stocks, stews, vegetables and soups. The classic combination is parsley, thyme and a bay leaf, with twice as much parsley used as the other two herbs. The bunch is tied with a long piece of string which can be attached to the handle of the saucepan so that it can be easily removed at the end of the cooking time.

Bouquet garnis can also be made with finely chopped herbs which are enclosed in a small square of muslin. Again, the muslin is tied with a long piece of string. If you use muslin, you can also add other flavourings, such as dried citrus peel or cloves of garlic.

The herbs included in bouquet garnis can vary according to your taste and the dish you are cooking. Other good combinations of herbs are:

Parsley, chives and thyme (for poultry dishes)
Parsley, rosemary, bay and juniper (for game dishes)
Parsley, bay and lemon thyme (for lamb dishes)
Parsley, bay, sage, marjoram and lemon peel (for lamb dishes)
Parsley, bay, thyme and citrus peel (for pork dishes)
Parsley, bay, thyme and cloves (for beef dishes)

Waterzoi

Serves 4-6

This Dutch fish soup adapts well to microwave cooking. The stock, flavoured with a bouquet garni made up of a bay leaf, thyme and parsley, can be made in advance and frozen for later use.

450 g (1 lb) white fish, such as turbot, monkfish or cod, or freshwater fish, such as pike or perch, skin and bones reserved.
Bouquet garni
6 black peppercorns
1 tbsp lemon juice
2 shallots, finely chopped
140 ml (¼pint) dry white wine
120 g (4 oz) carrots, cut into thin rounds
2 sticks celery, thinly sliced
2 leeks, well washed and cut into thin rounds
Salt and freshly ground black pepper
200 ml (7 fl oz) double cream
3 tbsp chopped parsley, to garnish

1 Combine the fish bones and trimmings with 430 ml (¾ pint) water, the bouquet garni, black peppercorns and lemon juice in a large, deep bowl. Cook in the microwave on HIGH for 10 minutes and then strain.

2 Discard the bouquet garni and the fish bones and trimmings.

3 Combine this fish stock with the wine, shallots, carrots, celery and leeks in a large bowl. Cover loosely and cook for about 6 minutes on HIGH, or until the vegetables are nearly tender.

4 Cut the fish into 5 cm (2 in) pieces and add to the bowl. Season with salt and pepper, re-cover the bowl and cook for a further 6-8 minutes on HIGH or until cooked.

5 Stir in the double cream and leave the soup to stand for 2 minutes before serving.

6 Top each bowl with a sprinkling of chopped parsley before serving. The soup should be thin.

Lemon Balm

Lemon balm (Melissa officinalis) is a small, aromatic evergreen herb. Its pale green or variegated leaves both taste and smell of lemon. Lemon balm is often known by its botanical name, melissa (the Greek word for bee) as bees are attracted by its scent. It grows to a height of 60-100 cm (2-3 ft) and prefers poor, moist soil and a sunny position. Pale yellow or white flowers bloom throughout the summer. Although the plant dies down in winter, its root is perennial. Lemon balm is frequently used freshly chopped in salads or added to soups and egg dishes. It also partners fish well. Fresh lemon balm leaves makes a refreshing tea, either served hot with a dash of honey or cold poured over ice cubes, or mixed with sage (see recipe). Lemon balm leaves are excellent added to pot pourris as they keep their scent when dried.

July

8

The word balm is an abbreviation of balsam, the main sweet-smelling oil.

9

10

11

Lemon balm tea is said to relieve colds, as it encourages perspiration.

12

13

14

'As sweet as balm, as soft as air, as gently.'

Antony and Cleopatra
William Shakespeare

Sage-leaf Tea

For a refreshing tea, infuse 2 teaspoons fresh sage, 2 teaspoons fresh lemon balm, 3 teaspoons sugar and 2 lemon quarters in 600 ml (1 pint) hot water for 5 minutes. Strain and cool the liquid, then add 150 ml (5 fl oz) white wine.

Contented Cows

If lemon balm is grown in meadows and pastures, it is said to improve the flow of milk in cows grazing there. A brew of lemon balm and marjoram can be given to cows after calving to help them regain their strength and to soothe them.

Oranges with Lemon Balm

Serves 4

The citrus taste of lemon balm makes it the perfect herb to accompany oranges flavoured with Grand Marnier.

4 oranges
140 ml (¼ pint) sweet white wine
15-30 ml (1-2 tbsp) honey
15 ml (1 tbsp) Grand Marnier
1 tsp chopped lemon balm
Whole lemon balm leaves, to garnish

1 Peel the oranges, removing all the white pith. Cut the oranges into slices and arrange on a serving dish.

2 Mix the wine, honey to taste and Grand Marnier together in a small bowl, stir in the lemon balm and microwave on HIGH for 2 minutes.

3 Stir to dissolve the honey and cook on MEDIUM for 5 minutes or until slightly reduced and syrupy.

4 Pour over the oranges and chill thoroughly. Garnish with whole lemon balm leaves.

'An essence of balm, given in canary wine every morning, will renew youth, strengthen the brain, relieve languishing nature and prevent baldness.'

The London Dispensary, 1696

Flat-leaf Parsley

Flat-leaf or French parsley (*Petroselinum crispum*) is grown mainly for flavour, while its curly-leafed cousin is grown for use as a garnish. It is rich in vitamin C. Although parsley does not dry well, it can be frozen – pack it into plastic bags, squeeze out as much air as possible and freeze. Flat-leaf parsley will grow in a sunny position in a rich, moist soil and is an ideal herb for container growing, either indoors or outdoors. There are various varieties available, from dwarf plants to those which can grow to over 60 cm (2 ft) in height.

According to country folklore, parsley should only be sown on Good Friday, when the soil is free from the powers of Satan. As it is slow to germinate, this is believed to speed its growth. It is thought to be unlucky to give parsley away, particularly with its root. Avoid bad luck by pointing out the spot where it is growing and allow the recipient to help himself.

Parsley is able to absorb other flavours. After deep-frying fish or seafood, fry several sprigs of parsley in the oil and the fishy flavour will disappear.

July

15

16

Hot parsley tea works as a tonic and is believed to relieve rheumatism pains.

17

18

19

20

21

Herb Mustards

Give mustards a different flavour by adding fresh herbs, such as tarragon, dill or parsley. Make the mustard just before it is required in order to get the full flavour.

Herb Cheese Balls

These decorative cheese balls are ideal to serve as part of a cheese course. Serve them on a bed of fresh vine leaves with grapes.

Mix 225 g (8 oz) low-fat soft cheese with 100 g (4 oz) finely grated Cheshire cheese and 3 tablespoons of finely chopped fresh herbs, such as parsley, chives or basil. Chill the mixture in the refrigerator for 2 hours or until firm. Shape the mixture into small balls, about 2.5 cm (1 in) in diameter, by rolling them between damp hands. Roll each ball in chopped herbs to coat thoroughly. Chill until ready to serve.

Mixed Herb Mustard

50 g (2 oz) mustard powder
1½ tsp sugar
½ tsp salt
40 ml (1½ fl oz) cider vinegar
3 tsp chopped fresh parsley
3 tsp chopped fresh thyme
40 ml (1½ fl oz) olive oil

Mix all the ingredients, except the olive oil, together in a food processor or blender. When the sugar has dissolved, add the oil slowly and mix until it is incorporated into the mustard.

Chives

Chives (Allium schoenoprasum) are one of the most common herbs and are often used for garnishing food. They are the smallest members of the onion family and date back to early Roman times. They grow in clumps with bright green, thin cylindrical stems topped with large pink or purple pompom flowers in midsummer. If the chives are to be used for cooking rather than purely decorative purposes, snip off the flowers to keep the oniony flavour in the leaves.

Chives prefer a rich, damp soil and should be grown in a sunny position. They are ideal for growing in containers as they grow to a height of 15-25 cm (6-10 in), but make sure they do not dry out. Chives are perennial plants, growing from bulbs. The clumps of bulbs can be dug up and divided either in spring or autumn.

July

22

Better is a dinner of herbs where love is, than
a stalled ox and hatred therewith.

Proverbs 17

23

24

25

26

27

Grow chives around the roots of an apple tree
to improve the health of the tree.

28

Hot Tomato Salad

Serves 4

This recipe takes only minutes to prepare and cook in the microwave, yet it looks and tastes sensational, either as a starter or as a side dish to accompany grilled fish or chicken. For a warming light meal or snack, serve the hot tomatoes with crusty bread or rolls and cheese. If basil is not available, replace with other herbs such as marjoram or dill. Be careful that the tomatoes do not overcook and fall apart.

2 large beef tomatoes (total weight about 560 g/1¼ lb)
3 tbsp olive oil
1 tbsp cider vinegar
1 tsp chopped chives
1 tsp roughly chopped basil
½ tsp wholegrain mustard

1 Slice the tomatoes and arrange in a large microproof serving dish or four individual dishes.

2 Mix the oil, vinegar, chives, basil and mustard in a small jug and pour over the tomatoes.

3 Cook, uncovered, on HIGH for 2-3 minutes until hot but not cooked. If using individual dishes, arrange these in a circle in the microwave. Check the tomatoes frequently during the cooking time and baste them occasionally with the dressing. Serve immediately.

Lemon and Chive Butter

Mix butter with lemon and chives and use to flavour new potatoes, steamed vegetables or simply spread on warm French bread for a tasty snack. Mix 120 g (4 oz) slightly softened butter with 1 tbsp finely chopped chives, the zest of ¼ lemon and a few drops of lemon juice.

Lavender

Lavender (Lavandula angustifolia) is the traditional Victorian fragrance. There are many varieties of lavender, the commonest being the purple English lavender and the paler French variety. A hardy, evergreen shrub, it grows as a compact bush up to 75 cm (30 in) in height and will thrive in poor but well-drained soil in a sunny position. It is a herb of Mediterranean origins and the fields of lavender found in the south of France are a breathtaking sight.

Lavender was once used for all sorts of cosmetic purposes and its heady fragrance scented Victorian parlours, bedrooms and drawing rooms. Linen chests and cupboards were perfumed with lavender sachets and lavender shrubs were often grown near the kitchen door so newly washed clothes could be spread over them to dry.

July

29

Oil of lavender rubbed on the skin is said to prevent midge and mosquito bites,

30

31

'Who'll buy my lavender, fresh lavender,
Sweet blooming lavender, who'll buy?'

The call of a nineteenth-century lavender seller

Lavender Scented Pillows

These sweetly scented pillows make ideal presents. They are easy to sew and use up small fabric remnants. These two cushions have been made in shades of lavender and blue, but if you are making them as gifts, you could choose fabrics in shades of the recipient's favourite colour. Both pillows are made in a log cabin patchwork pattern, varying the size of the central patch. In a traditional log cabin design, darker fabrics are used on two adjoining sides of the cushion, while lighter colours are used on the opposite sides. The scented pillows can be as large or small as you wish.

You will need:

Small strips of fabric in coordinating colours
Terylene wadding
Ribbon
Dried lavender

1 Cut out a square of fabric to form the centre of the cushion. Working from the centre outwards, add strips of fabric to the sides of the central square. Continue sewing strips until the cushion front is the required size.

2 Cut out a square of fabric for the back of the cushion. Placing right sides together, sew the front and back together along three sides.

3 Turn right sides out. Stuff the cushion with wadding and add the lavender. This can either be sprinkled loose inside the cushion or, if you will want to wash the cushion at a later date, make a small fabric sachet, fill it with lavender and slip this inside the cushion.

4 Sew up the fourth side. If you have made a larger cushion that will need washing, you could add a zip or press studs.

5 Finally, stitch some ribbon bows to the front of the cushion, if desired.

Lavender Sugar

Sugar scented with the delicate fragrance of lavender is ideal for sprinkling on cakes and desserts. Simply mix either dried or fresh lavender flowers with sugar and place in a lidded container. Store in a warm place for 1-2 weeks, shaking the container occasionally to distribute the lavender amongst the sugar. Sift the sugar to remove the lavender heads and store the scented sugar in an airtight container. For 225 g (8 oz) of sugar, use either 30 g (1 oz) of dried lavender or 60 g (2oz) of fresh.

Lavender can also be used to flavour vinegars, honey and various sweet desserts, such as ice creams and custards.

August

Feverfew

Feverfew (Chrysanthemum parthenium) is also known by the wonderful names of Flirtwort and Bachelor's Button. As well as being a fairly common garden plant, it can also be found growing in hedgerows and meadows. It has lacy yellow or green leaves and distinctive, daisy-like yellow and white flowers which bloom from early summer. It will thrive in a well drained, moist soil and full sunlight, reaching a height of 45-60 cm (18-24 in). It is a hardy perennial and requires little attention in the garden, producing masses of blooms year after year. Unlike many other flowering herbs, feverfew is one herb disliked by bees.

Feverfew's aromatic leaves are not often used in cooking due to their bitter taste. However, they have been proved to be effective in curing headaches and migraines. The leaves can be shredded and added to salads or made into a tea which has a slight sedative effect.

August

1

2

According to folklore, feverfew planted around the house will ward off disease.

3

4

Sprigs of feverfew bound to the wrists are said to relieve fever.

5

6

7

Herb Oils

Herb oils are easy to make, pretty to look at, endlessly useful in cooking and make delightful gifts for adventurous cooks. The corks can be sealed with wax if you wish.

Buy the best oil you can – ideally extra virgin olive oil, but sunflower, safflower and groundnut oils can also be used. Decant a little oil from the bottle into a jug and add your chosen herbs to the bottle. Pour back the reserved oil and seal and label the bottle. Keep the bottle in a warm place for several weeks to allow the oil to absorb the flavour of the herb. Strain the oil, return to the clean bottle, seal and store in a cool cupboard until required.

Make up your own recipes for flavouring oils using your favourite herbs. The following herbs are particularly recommended, but experiment with different combinations.

Basil, bay, chervil, dill, fennel, lavender, lovage, marjoram, mint, parsley, rosemary, sage, thyme.

You can also add peeled cloves of garlic, peppercorns of various colours, fresh chillies, allspice berries, juniper berries and strips of orange or lemon peel.

If making basil oil, pound the basil leaves in a pestle and mortar to release the flavour before adding to the oil.

Feta Cheese in Oil

Feta cheese is traditionally made from ewes' milk but varieties are also available made from goats' milk. Originally from Greece, it is a crumbly, white cheese with a sharp flavour. It is often crumbled or cubed and served in a Greek salad with black olives. When preserved in oil and herbs, it takes on their additional flavour.

Slice the feta cheese into even-sized cubes and place in a wide-necked storage jar. Pour in enough olive oil to cover the cheese completely. Add several sprigs of rosemary, slivers of red pepper, a garlic clove or two and some peppercorns. When the cheese has been eaten, use the oil in cooking.

Herb Cheese

Make your own cheese using runny yogurt and plenty of fresh herbs. Tarragon and chives work well in this recipe.

454 g (16 oz) carton low-fat natural yogurt
½ tsp salt
2 tsp chopped fresh herbs
1 clove garlic, peeled and crushed
Freshly ground black pepper
10 ml (2 tsp) olive oil

1 Line a nylon sieve with kitchen paper and sit it over a large bowl. Mix the yogurt and salt and pour into the sieve. Place the sieve and bowl in the refrigerator for 24 hours or until the yogurt is firm and the whey has drained into the bowl.

2 Place the yogurt in a bowl and add the herbs, garlic and season to taste. Mix well and place in a serving bowl. Drizzle oil over the top of the cheese.

Silver Thyme

As its name suggests, silver thyme (Thymus x citriodorus 'Silver Queen') has leaves which are a silvery-grey in colour, rather than the more common green leaves of garden thyme. It is one of the hardiest thyme varieties. It produces small, scented lilac flowers in summer and grows to a height of 10 cm (4 in).

The thyme botanical family is a very large group, with over 60 European species alone. The different species are known by some beautifully descriptive names, including orange thyme, caraway thyme, running thyme, mother of thyme.

According to Roman custom, the fragrance of wild thyme was believed to lift the spirits and it was prescribed to people suffering from depression. An extraction of thyme, thymol, was once used as a disinfectant as it is more powerful than carbolic acid and less irritating to the skin.

August

8

9

10

11

12

In the sixteenth century, thyme was believed to 'cure sciatica and pains in the head'.

13

14

Olives are often flavoured by placing sprigs of thyme in their oil.

Herb Rice Pilaff

Fresh herbs are essential for this dish, but use whatever mixture suits your taste or complements the main course. Serve the pilaff as a side dish to accompany meat, poultry or game.

30 ml (2 tbsp) oil
30 g (2 tbsp) butter
180 g (6 oz) uncooked long grain rice
570 ml (1 pint) boiling water
Pinch of salt and freshly ground black pepper
90 g (3 oz) finely chopped fresh herbs (parsley, thyme, marjoram, basil)
1 small bunch of spring onions, finely chopped

1 Heat the oil in a large, heavy-based saucepan and add the butter. When foaming, add the rice and cook over a moderate heat for about 2 minutes, stirring constantly.

2 When the rice begins to look opaque, add the water, salt and pepper and bring to the boil, stirring occasionally.

3 Cover the pan and reduce the heat. Simmer very gently, without stirring, for about 20 minutes or until all the liquid has been absorbed and the rice is tender. Add extra liquid or pour some off as necessary during cooking.

4 Stir the herbs and spring onions into the rice. Cover the pan and leave to stand for about 5 minutes before serving.

Summer Straw Hat

Transform a simple straw hat into elegant headwear suitable for a summer wedding. Choose a selection of herbs, both leaves and flowers, in colours to match your outfit. The herbs used here include parsley, dill and feverfew. Do not decorate the hat too far in advance of wearing it as the herbs will begin to wilt after a while.

1 Separate the herbs into small sprigs with fairly long stems and stand in water until required.

2 Position small bunches of herbs at the base of the crown. Attach the sprigs to the hat with a needle and cotton. Push the needle through from the inside of the hat, loop the cotton over the stalks and pass the needle through the straw again to the inside. The cotton can then be tied in a tight knot to secure the herbs.

3 Alternatively, attach a wide strip of ribbon in a coordinating colour around the base of the crown. Attach to the hat with a few stitches here and there. The herb sprigs can then be sewn onto the ribbon.

4 The sprigs of herbs should all be laid in the same direction, so the flowers or foliage of one bunch overlap and hide the stalks of the previous bunch.

5 Keep the hat in a cool place until you are ready to wear it.

Catmint

Catmint (*Nepeta cataria*), also known as catnip, belongs to the same botanical family as mint and nettles. It is native to Europe and parts of Asia and can also be found in North America. It grows wild in hedgerows, wasteground, on roadsides and at field edges, particularly where the soil is chalky. Catmint grows to a height of 60-90 cm (2-3 ft), with grey-green leaves and pale pink, white or lilac flowers which bloom from midsummer.

The plant has a smell similar to that of pennyroyal. It is this scent, given off when the leaves are bruised, which attracts cats, and dried catmint leaves are often used in small soft toys made for cats to play with.

The fresh leaves are a good source of vitamin C and can be used to make a refreshing tisane. The young, green shoots can be chopped and added to salads.

August

15

16

The juice of catmint drunk in wine is said to be good for bruises.

17

18

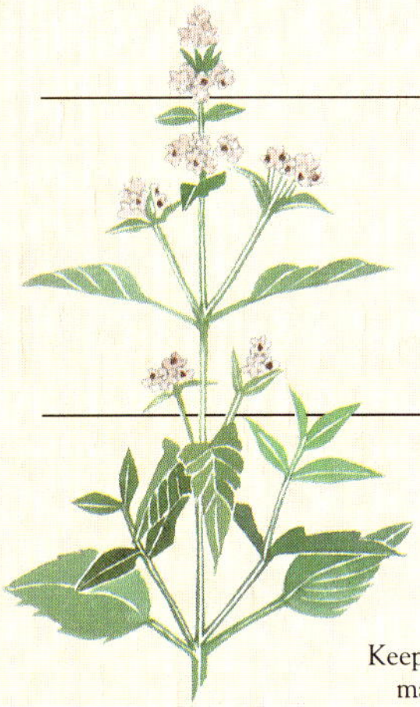

19

20

Keep nightmares at bay by eating conserve made from the young tops of catmint.

21

Scented Coat Hanger

Transform a plain, everyday wooden coat hanger into something special. The small hearts hanging from it are filled with dried lavender which has a dual purpose – both scenting the wardrobe and keeping moths at bay.

You will need:

Wooden coat hanger
Strips of wadding
Cotton fabric 85 x 15 cm (34 x 6 in)
Dried lavender
Ribbon
Two small buttons

1 Cover the coat hanger with strips of wadding. Wrap them around the hanger like a bandage until it is well padded. Secure the ends of the wadding with a few small stitches.

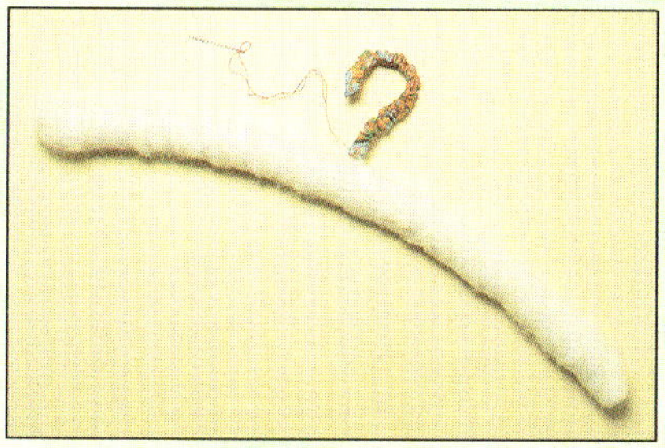

2 Cut a piece of fabric 25 x 4 cm (10 x 1½ in). Fold in half lengthwise, with right sides facing, and stitch across one end.

3 Turn the fabric right side out and stitch along the long edge with a simple running stitch. Gather the fabric sleeve by pulling the threads gently. Slip the sleeve over the coat hanger hook and attach at the base to the wadding with a few stitches.

4 Cut a piece of fabric 60 x 15 cm (24 x 6 in). Fold in half lengthwise, wrong sides facing. Fold a 1.25 cm (½ in) hem and press along the fold line. Sew up the two short ends.

5 Slip the fabric sleeve over the padding, with the open edge uppermost. Pin the top seams together, making sure the fabric is evenly gathered along the length of the coat hanger. Stitch the seam 6 mm (¼ in) from the top edge.

6 Cut four hearts of the same size from the remaining piece of fabric. Place two hearts, right sides facing, and sew together, leaving a small opening in the centre of the top. Turn right sides out, fill the heart with lavender and complete the seam. Attach a length of ribbon and a decorative button. Repeat to make the other heart, but attach a slightly shorter piece of ribbon.

Lemon Verbena

Lemon verbena (Lippia citriodora) is a fragrant, perennial shrub from South America. It can grow to a height of 1.5 m (5 ft) if planted in a warm, sheltered spot, but can also be grown indoors as a pot plant. This herb can survive in poor, dry soil, but needs to be protected from harsh winter weather.

In midsummer, lemon verbena produces masses of pale purple or white flowers. Its slender green leaves smell strongly of lemon and they can be used fresh in fruit salads, punches and fruit cups, or dried and added to pot pourris. The leaves can also be added to home-made ice creams or used to flavour oils and vinegars. Add the leaves sparingly as they have a powerful flavour.

Oil extracted from lemon verbena leaves is widely used by perfumers. This plant is also known as Herb Louisa.

August

22

A mouthwash made from an infusion of lemon verbena is said to strengthen gums and help prevent tooth decay.

23

24

25

Dried lemon verbena leaves keep their scent for years and are ideal for pot pourri mixtures.

26

27

28

Herbal Beauty Products

It is very easy to make chemical-free beauty products using herbs to suit your own type of skin. Herbs are particularly good for looking after oily skins. Many of the ingredients needed can be found in the kitchen storecupboard. Store lotions in the refrigerator if they are not to be used immediately.

All lotions should be used within a couple of days.

Sage and Peppermint Facial Steam

This will improve circulation and cleanse the skin. It is not suitable for dry skins. First, wash or cleanse your face. Fill a large bowl with approximately 1 litre (2 pints) boiling water and add 2 tbsp freshly chopped sage and 2 tbsp freshly chopped peppermint. Hold your head about 30 cm (12 in) above the bowl and cover with a large towel to prevent the steam escaping. After 10 minutes gently pat your face with a face cloth rinsed out in cold water.

Marigold Hand Oil

Mix 250 ml (8 fl oz) sweet almond oil with 25 g (1 oz) fresh marigold petals. Pour into a clean, screwtop jar and leave in a warm place for 3 weeks, shaking the bottle daily. Pour the oil into a saucepan and heat gently until the marigold petals become crisp. Strain the oil and pour into a clean jar. Rub a little oil into the hands daily.

Peppermint Face Mask

This mask is for a greasy skin as it is extremely drying. Place 1 egg white with ¼ tsp kaolin in a bowl and mix to a paste. Stir in ¼ tsp of peppermint extract and add enough water to make the mask the right consistency.

Lemon Verbena Tea

The leaves of the lemon verbena plant make a refreshing tisane which also has a mild sedative effect. Either fresh or dried leaves can be used.

Apple and Mint Astringent

This astringent will improve the texture of the skin and add colour. Place 3 tsp chopped fresh mint and 2 tbsp apple cider vinegar in a screwtop jar. Leave for 7 days. Strain the liquid into a bowl and add 285 ml (½ pint) soft water. Stir well, pour into clean jars and store in a cool place.

Tarragon

French tarragon (*Artemesia dracunculus*) is one of the best herbs for cooking. A bushy, perennial herb, tarragon grows in sunny positions and in good, well drained soil to a height of 1 m (3 ft). It also grows well in pots and containers. Tarragon has slender, aromatic green leaves and produces small white flowers in late summer. Fresh tarragon can be added to salads and vegetable dishes.

Tarragon vinegar is made by infusing herbs in bottles of white wine vinegar and can be used in salad dressings.

Russian tarragon has larger, paler leaves, but its taste is inferior to that of French tarragon.

August

29

30

Tarragon is one of the 'Dragon Herbs', said to have the power to heal the bites of mad dogs and the stings of venomous beasts.

31

The root of tarragon was once used to cure toothache.

Chicken and Avocado Salad

Serves 4

This creamy herb dressing is the ideal partner for chicken and avocado. The dressing can be prepared in advance and stored in the refrigerator for several days. It can also be used as a dip for vegetable crudités or with a tossed salad.

8 anchovy fillets, soaked in milk, rinsed and dried
1 spring onion, chopped
2 tbsp chopped fresh tarragon
3 tbsp chopped chives
4 tbsp chopped parsley
280 ml (½ pint) prepared mayonnaise
140 ml (¼ pint) natural yogurt
30 ml (2 tbsp) tarragon vinegar
Pinch of sugar and cayenne pepper
1 large head of lettuce
450 g (1 lb) cooked chicken
1 avocado, peeled and sliced or cubed
15 ml (1 tbsp) lemon juice

1 Combine all the ingredients except the lettuce, chicken, avocado and lemon juice in a food processor or with a hand blender. Blend the ingredients until smooth and well mixed. Leave in the refrigerator for at least 1 hour for the flavours to blend.

2 Shred the lettuce or tear into bite-sized pieces and arrange on plates.

3 Top the lettuce with the cooked chicken cut into cubes or strips.

4 Spoon the dressing over the chicken. Brush the avocado slices or toss the cubes with the lemon juice and garnish the salad. Serve any remaining dressing separately.

Tarragon is the perfect partner for chicken; poulet à l'estragon is a classic French dish. It can also be used to add flavour to egg and fish dishes and to make sauces, such as tartar sauce.

Tarragon and Lemon Carrots

Serves 4

Tarragon makes a lovely alternative to the more traditional mint in this recipe.

450 g (1 lb) carrots, finely sliced
1 tbsp lemon juice
6 tbsp water
2 sprigs fresh tarragon
Chopped tarragon, to garnish
Grated lemon zest, to garnish

1 Put the carrots in a casserole dish with the lemon juice, water and tarragon sprigs. Cover and cook in the microwave on HIGH for 10-12 minutes.

2 Drain the carrots and discard the tarragon sprigs. Place the carrots in a serving dish and garnish with the chopped tarragon and lemon zest.

'Tarragon is highly cordial and friend to the head, heart and liver.'

John Evelyn

Tarragon Mustard

50 g (2 oz) black mustard seeds
3 tsp flour
½ tsp salt
1½ tsp honey
50 ml (2 fl oz) tarragon vinegar
2 tsp chopped fresh tarragon

Grind the mustard seeds. Mix with a little cold water and leave for 10 minutes for the flavour to develop. Put the mustard and the other ingredients in a food processor or blend and mix thoroughly.

September

Comfrey

Comfrey (Symphytum officinale) is a hardy perennial with long, coarse, grey-green leaves with blue or cream flowers which bloom throughout the summer. It is a member of the borage family. This is a tall, spreading plant, growing to a height of 60-90 cm (2-3 ft), which seeds itself. Comfrey will grow in almost any type of well drained, fertile soil. It is an excellent plant to add to composts as it speeds the breakdown of other compost plants.

Comfrey leaves and stalks are both used in cooking. The leaves, which are rich in minerals and vitamins, can be cooked like spinach or chopped and added to green salads (only use young leaves picked before they become too tough). The stalks can be blanched and cooked like asparagus.

Comfrey has been widely used for medicinal purposes in the past. Its leaves and roots can be made into a cough mixture and it can be used to treat all kinds of lung ailments.

September

1

2

Comfrey is also known as Bruisewort, Knitbone and Boneset due to its curative properties.

3

4

5

The roots of comfrey, chicory and dandelion can be brewed together to make a drink tasting similar to coffee.

6

7

Comfrey roots can be made into a poultice for treating bruises and swellings.

Lavender Water

Lavender water is a delightfully old-fashioned cologne which is very refreshing to use on hot summer days. The best alcohol to use is vodka, as it is unscented and will not detract from the lavender.

Pour 285 ml (½ pint) alcohol into a clean bottle. Add 1 tsp lavender oil and 6 tbsp rosewater. Shake well and place in a cool, dark cupboard. Shake the bottle every day for a month and then decant into pretty perfume bottles. The lavender water can be used after one month, but the fragrance will improve if it is left for longer.

Pot Pourri Parcel

It is now possible to buy sheets of beautiful hand-made papers in most craft shops and stationers. These papers are available in a wide variety of colours and textures, some are even made with herb petals and leaves rolled into the paper. These sheets are ideal for making small envelopes to hold scented pot pourri which can be placed in drawers and closets. The sachets are very easy to make once you have mastered the folding sequence. You may like to practise first with a piece of scrap paper.

You will need:

Sheet of hand-made paper
Double-sided adhesive tape or glue
Craft knife
Narrow ribbon
Pot pourri or lavender

1 Cut out a rectangle of paper approximately 25 x 21 cm (10 x 8¼ in). Fold the two shorter sides into the centre and overlap by about 1 cm (½ in). Fold over one of the ends by about 1 cm (½ in). You will now have a long sachet open at one end.

2 At the open end, trim away one side so that you have a flap which can fold over to seal the sachet.

3 Using the glue or tape, stick the bottom flap and the central front seam.

4 With a craft knife, cut 2 small slits through the flap. These are the holes the ribbon will thread through to close the sachet.

5 Close the flap and make corresponding slits in the actual sachet so that the ribbon can slip through all the sachet layers.

6 Fill the sachet with pot pourri, thread the ribbon through the slits and tie.

Coriander

Coriander (Coriandrum sativum) is an easy-to-grow hardy annual. Growing to a height of 60 cm (2 ft), it prefers a sunny position and light, rich soil. Its lower leaves are bright green and look similar to flat-leaf parsley, while the upper leaves are more feathery, with small, pinkish-white flowers. This is one of the oldest herbs, grown mainly for its seeds which have a mild flavour. However, until the seeds ripen, the whole plant has an unpleasant smell. For this reason, it is best not to grow it too close to the kitchen door! The leaves have a sharp taste and can be added to green salads and vegetables dishes.

Coriander originally comes from the East and was introduced to Europe by the Romans. It is still widely used in the cooking of India and Thailand.

Coriander is used in medicine mainly to disguise unpleasant tastes.

September

8

In ancient times the Chinese believed one of the powers of coriander was immortality.

9

10

11

An Anglo-Saxon recipe for a hand cream to treat chapped, rough hands was a poultice of beet, lettuce, coriander and crumbs, mixed to a paste with water.

12

13

14

Coriander is widely cultivated in Peru and is used to flavour many of their dishes, including a soup made from its leaves.

Chicken with 'Burnt' Peppers and Coriander

Serves 4

'Burning' peppers is a technique for removing the skins. This also imparts a delicious flavour which goes well with coriander. Serve the chicken with plain boiled rice.

2 red peppers, halved and seeded
1 green pepper, halved and seeded
60 ml (4 tbsp) vegetable oil, for brushing
15 ml (1 tbsp) olive oil
10 ml (1 tsp) paprika
1.25 ml (¼ tsp) ground cumin
Pinch of cayenne pepper
2 cloves garlic, peeled and crushed
450 g (1 lb) tinned tomatoes, drained and chopped
3 tbsp chopped fresh coriander
3 tbsp chopped fresh parsley
Salt
4 large chicken breasts, boned
1 large onion, sliced
60 g (2 oz) flaked almonds

1 Put the peppers, cut side down, on a flat surface and gently press them with the palm of your hand to flatten them out.

2 Brush the skin side with 30 ml (2 tbsp) of the vegetable oil and cook them, skin side up, under a hot grill until the skin chars and splits. Wrap the peppers in a clean tea towel for 10 minutes to cool.

3 Unwrap the peppers and carefully peel off the charred skin. Chop the pepper flesh into thin strips.

4 Heat the olive oil in a frying pan and gently fry the paprika, cayenne pepper and garlic for 2 minutes, stirring to prevent the garlic burning. Stir in the tomatoes and herbs and season with salt. Simmer for 15-20 minutes or until thick. Set aside.

5 Heat the remaining vegetable oil in an ovenproof dish and sauté the chicken breasts, turning them frequently until they are golden brown on both sides.

6 Remove the chicken and set aside. Gently fry the onions in the oil for about 5 minutes or until softened but not overcooked. Return the chicken to the casserole with the onions and pour on about 280 ml (½ pint) water. Bring to the boil. Cover the casserole and simmer for about 30 minutes, turning the chicken occasionally to prevent it burning.

7 Remove the chicken from the casserole and boil the remaining liquid rapidly to reduce to about 90 ml (3 fl oz) of stock. Add the peppers and the tomato sauce to the stock and stir well.

8 Return the chicken to the casserole, cover and simmer gently for 30 minutes or until the chicken is tender. Spoon the chicken on to a serving dish with the sauce and sprinkle with almonds.

Coriander Seeds

Harvest coriander seeds in late summer. Cut off the seedheads when they have turned brown. Leave them to dry in a warm, airy place for several days. When the seedheads are completely dry, shake out the seeds and store in a jar. Coriander seeds have a mild, citrus flavour and can either be used whole in fish dishes or in baking, or ground and added to curry powder. The coriander seeds are also used to add flavour to alcoholic spirits, such as gin.

Hyssop

Hyssop (Hyssopus officinalis) is a hardy evergreen perennial. It has aromatic, dark green leaves and woody stems, and during its long growing season produces pink, blue and white flowers. Hyssop grows to a height of 30-60 cm (1-2 ft) and is ideal to grow in a container. It prefers a sunny position and light, well drained soil.

Hyssop is one of the oldest herbs and is known as a holy herb because it was once used to clean sacred buildings. It is mentioned in the Bible in this connection.

Hyssop has a strong, minty taste and smell and was once used in preserving meat. Hyssop tea, sweetened with honey, was once used to relieve rheumatic pains and to encourage perspiration. It is also helpful in treating chest ailments. An infusion of hyssop makes a good expectorant. Fresh hyssop leaves can be added to green salads or vegetable soups.

September

15

16

Bees are attracted to hyssop because of its minty aroma, producing pleasant tasting honey.

17

18

Hyssop is one of the herbs used to flavour the liqueur chartreuse.

19

20

21

French cooks use sprigs of hyssop to add extra flavour to tomato preserves.

Muslin Bath Sachets

Give yourself a bathtime treat with these bath sachets. They are filled with a mixture of herbs which will both scent the bath water and relax you after a stressful day. The muslin can be dyed with cold water dyes if you wish. These sachets also make ideal presents.

You will need:

Remnants of muslin
Lengths of narrow ribbon in coordinating colours
Oatmeal
Powdered milk
Mixed dried herbs, such as rosemary, lavender, thyme or marjoram

1 For each bag, cut out a piece of muslin 10 x 15 cm (4 x 6 in).

2 Fold muslin in half lengthwise and sew the bottom and side seams to make a sachet. Trim the top edge with pinking shears.

3 Turn the sachet inside out (so that the seams are on the inside).

4 In a large bowl mix together equal quantities of oatmeal and powdered milk and sufficient herbs to scent the mixture. Fill the sachets half-full with this mixture.

5 Tie a matching ribbon around the top of the sachet and loop the ribbon over the bath tap so that the bath water will run through the sachet.

Ring-a-ring o' roses
A pocket full of posies
Atishoo, atishoo, we all fall down

This popular children's nursery rhyme dates back to 1664 – the year of the Great Plague of London. The posies were the 'magic' herbs which were carried in the pocket and were thought to ward off the virus. The herbs included hyssop, rosemary, thyme and southernwood. They were also used to disguise the unpleasant smells of the plague.

Pineapple Mint

Pineapple mint (Mentha suaveolens variegata) is a variety of apple mint, but has green and white variegated leaves which make it a pretty herb to grow in the garden and perfect as a food garnish. A perennial plant, it produces long spikes of pale white or cream flowers.

Pineapple mint grows to a height of 20-30 cm (8-12 in) and prefers partial shade and a moist, rich soil. As its name suggests, it has a pleasant pineapple flavour and the leaves are ideal to add to fruit cups and punches. Pineapple mint leaves make a good addition to pot pourris, particularly those with a fruity scent, such as a mix of lemon verbena, apple mint and other herbs with similar scents.

Like all mints, it is an invasive plant which can take over a whole garden if it is not kept strictly under control. It is therefore a good herb for container growing.

September

22

23

24

'Here did she fall a tear; here, in this place,
I'll set a bank of rue, sour herb of grace.'

Richard II
William Shakespeare

25

26

27

28

In ancient Greece mint was a symbol of hospitality and tables were traditionally rubbed with it before being set for dinner guests.

Chicken Liver Pâté with Parsley and Coriander

Serves 4

This smooth pâté has a rich flavour and can either be served as a snack with toast or as a more substantial ploughman's lunch with French bread and salad.

450 g (1 lb) chicken livers, trimmed
225 g (8 oz) butter
4 shallots, finely chopped
2 cloves garlic, peeled and chopped
½ tsp ground coriander
2 tsp chopped fresh parsley
Salt and freshly ground black pepper
10 ml (2 tsp) mango chutney
120 g (4 oz) clarified butter, to garnish (see below)
Coriander leaves, to garnish

1 If the livers are large, cut them into even-sized pieces. Melt half the butter in a sauté pan and add the liver, shallots, garlic and coriander. Cook over a moderate heat until the livers are cooked through.

2 Allow to cool completely, then pureé in a food processor or blender. For a smoother pâté, push the mixture through a metal sieve.

3 Add the remaining butter, parsley, salt and pepper and chutney. Process the pâté again until smooth. Transfer to a serving dish.

4 To clarify the butter, melt 120 g (4 oz) butter in a small, heavy-based saucepan and bring it to a rapid boil. Remove from the heat and leave to settle for 30 minutes. Spoon off the clear butter oil from the top and discard the sediment. Spoon a layer of clarified butter over the top of the pâté to a thickness of about 1.25 cm (½ inch) and chill in the refrigerator until the butter solidifies. Garnish with fresh coriander leaves.

Fresh Herb Basket

A wicker basket filled with a selection of culinary herbs is a welcome gift for keen cooks, especially if they do not have their own herb garden.

Line the basket with a layer of plastic wrap. Pick bunches of herbs with fairly long stems and wrap them in dampened kitchen paper. Tightly pack the bunches into the basket. The herbs will stay fresh for a couple of days if the basket is kept in a cool place. The selection shown here includes rosemary, purple sage, chives, variegated mint, bronze fennel, common thyme and golden marjoram.

Soapwort

Soapwort (*Saponaria officinalis*) is an attractive herb with large, pale pink flowers which bloom from midsummer. It usually reaches to a height of 60 cm (2 ft), but can grow to 1.5 m (5 ft). It thrives in a sunny position and moist soil and often grows wild.

This herb is not scented, but the prettiness of its flowers make it well worth cultivating. It was once widely used on wash day and in laundries as the leaves macerated in water produce a gentle lather excellent for cleaning delicate fabrics. Boil the bruised roots, stems and leaves for 30 minutes in just enough water to cover them. Strain the liquid and add to the washing water.

Soapwort is also known by the wonderful country names of Bouncing Bet, Soaproot, Wild Sweet William, Sweet Betty and Latherwort.

September

29

Soapwort was once used to cure various ailments, including jaundice and rheumatism.

30

Spiced Oranges with Honey and Mint

Serves 4

An unusual combination of flavours blend to create this light and very refreshing dessert. Ruby grapefruit can be substituted for the oranges if you wish.

280 ml (½ pint) clear honey
430 ml (¾ pint) water
2 large sprigs fresh mint
12 whole cloves
4 large oranges
Small sprigs of mint, to garnish

1 Put the honey and water into a heavy-based saucepan. Add the mint and cloves and slowly bring to the boil. Stir the mixture to dissolve the honey and boil rapidly for 5 minutes or until the liquid is very syrupy.

2 Leave the mixture to cool completely, then strain the syrup through a nylon sieve into a jug or bowl to remove the mint sprigs and the cloves.

3 Using a potato peeler, carefully pare the rind very thinly from one orange. Cut the pared rind into very fine shreds with a sharp knife.

4 Put the shreds of orange peel into a small bowl and cover with boiling water. Allow to stand until cold, then drain, reserving only the peel.

5 Stir the peel into the honey syrup and chill well.

6 Peel the oranges, removing all the skin and especially the white pith. Slice the oranges into thin rounds using a sharp knife.

7 Arrange the orange rounds on four individual serving plates. Pour the chilled syrup over the orange and garnish with small sprigs of mint just before serving.

Rather than buying expensive flowers from a florist for decorative table centres, gather masses of fresh herbs (both flowers and foliage). Set a small glass vase crammed with aromatic herbs by each place setting to delight the senses of sight and smell. At times of the year when herb flowers are not in bloom, use herb leaves in various shades of silvery grey and green.

'For you there's rosemary and rue; these keep Seeming and savour all the winter long.'

The Winter's Tale
William Shakespeare

Flower Wreath

Capture the colours of summer in this bright and cheerful flower wreath. Here a wreath of florists' foam (also known as oasis) has been used. The bare wreath does not look as attractive as a cane or straw wreath but it has the added advantage that it can be soaked in water and the herbs are simply pushed into it. As their stems are in the damp foam, the wreath will last for quite a few days. If using florists' foam, be sure to cover all sides of the wreath so that none of the foam shows through.

The herbs used in this wreath include marigolds, nasturtiums, golden marjoram and fennel flowers.

October

Southernwood

Southernwood (Artemesia abrotanum) is a woody perennial shrub with grey-green feathery leaves which, when crushed, have a lemon scent. It sometimes produces small yellow flowers. It thrives in light, well drained soil in a sunny position and will grow to a height of 1 m (3 ft) if cut back each spring. It is a good plant for container growing.

With the exception of Italian cookery, southernwood is rarely used for culinary purposes, although a tisane can be made from its leaves. It represents the virtue of fidelity and was often included in country bouquets given to sweethearts.

Southernwood is said to ward off infection and was once widely used as an antiseptic. When dried, the feathery leaves can be added to linen sachets as they will keep away moths.

October

1

2

3

A hair tonic including southernwood was said to cure baldness, while an ointment made with its ashes was reputed to encourage the growth of a beard.

4

5

6

7

Country names for southernwood include lad's love, boy's love and old man.

Beef Casserole with Herb Dumplings

Serves 4

If fresh herbs are not available, substitute dried Herbes de Provence. This is a substantial, warming dish, ideal for feeding a hungry family. Using the microwave speeds up the cooking time enormously.

5 ml (1 tsp) oil
1 medium onion, peeled and finely chopped
340 g (12 oz) minced beef
30 g (1 oz) plain flour
140 ml (¼ pint) beef stock
15 ml (1 tbsp) tomato purée
Salt and freshly ground black pepper

Herb Dumplings
180 g (6 oz) plain flour
2.5 ml (½ tsp) baking powder
Pinch of dry mustard
60 g (2 oz) margarine
½ tsp chopped oregano
½ tsp chopped thyme
½ tsp chopped marjoram
70 ml (4½ tbsp) milk

1 Put the oil and the onion in a casserole and cook on HIGH for 3 minutes until soft.

2 Add the beef and cook on HIGH for 3-5 minutes, stirring occasionally. Stir in the flour, stock, tomato purée and seasoning.

3 To make the dumplings, sift the flour, baking powder, mustard and a pinch of salt into a mixing bowl. Rub in the margarine until the mixture resembles fine breadcrumbs and stir in the herbs. Add the milk gradually and mix to form a soft dough.

4 Divide the dough into eight balls and arrange around the edge of the casserole. Cover and cook on LOW for 10-15 minutes until the dumplings are cooked.

Herbes de Provence

Herbes de Provence is a blend of dried herbs from the Provence region of southern France. The classic mixture contains marjoram, thyme, rosemary, oregano and sage, and sometimes savory, mint, basil or fennel. They are used to flavour meat and vegetables dishes.

Broad Beans Provençal

Serves 4

This simple vegetable dish makes a good accompaniment to grilled or roast meats.

450 g (1 lb) fresh or frozen broad beans
30 g (2 tbsp) butter
2 tsp Herbes de Provence
4 tomatoes, seeded and diced
Salt and freshly ground black pepper

1 Cook the broad beans in boiling salted water for about 8 minutes or until tender. Drain and refresh under cold water. Peel off the outer skin if required.

2 Melt the butter and toss with the broad beans and dried herbs.

3 Heat the beans through and add the tomatoes, salt and pepper. Serve immediately.

Dill

Dill (Anethum graveolens) is a fragrant hardy annual with fine, feathery green leaves and small, deep yellow flowers. The flat heads of flowers can be up to 20 cm (8 in) in breadth.

A herb of Mediterranean origin, dill prefers a sunny position and fine, well drained soil. It will grow to a height of 60-90 cm (2-3 ft). The leaves are often used in a sauce to accompany fish or chopped and added to salads. Dill is the herb used in the Swedish dish of pickled raw salmon, gravlax. Dill seeds, harvested at the end of summer, can be used in stews, soups, vinegars and pickles.

The seeds scatter as soon as they are ripe, so the whole plant should be pulled up as soon as the flowerheads turn brown. Cut off the flowerheads and leave in a warm place to dry.

In the Middle Ages dill was used in magicians' spells and in witchcraft.

Nail Strengthener

Mash 4 tbsp fresh dill seed and pour a cup of boiling water over them. Leave the liquid to cool. Soak your fingernails in the liquid for 10 minutes and then pat dry.

October

8

9

Get a good night's sleep by drinking dill seed tea last thing at night.

10

11

'Therewith her vervain and her dill,
That hindreth witches of their will.'

Michael Drayton

12

13

Chew dill seeds to sweeten the breath.

14

Grilled Herrings with Dill

Serves 4

Dill and mustard give the herrings a delicious tangy flavour. Whole fresh mackerel can be used instead of herring. Serve the fish with new potatoes and a garnish of lemon wedges and dill.

4 tbsp chopped fresh dill
90 g (6 tbsp) mild mustard
30 ml (2 tbsp) lemon juice or white wine
4-8 herrings, cleaned but with heads and tails left on
25 g (1 oz) butter or margarine, melted
Salt and freshly ground black pepper
Lemon wedges and dill, to garnish

1 Mix the dill, mustard and lemon juice or wine together thoroughly.

2 Cut three slits, just piercing the skin, on both sides of the herring and lay them on a grill pan.

3 Spread half the mustard mixture equally over the exposed side of each fish, pushing some into the cuts.

4 Spoon a little of the melted butter over each herring and grill the fish for 5 minutes.

5 Turn the fish over and spread the remaining mustard mixture over them. Spoon over the remaining butter and grill for a further 5-6 minutes. Sprinkle the fish with a little salt and pepper before serving.

Dill Sauce

Dill is an excellent herb to serve with fish. This sauce can also be served hot or cold with vegetables.

25 g (2 oz) butter
1 tbsp flour
150 ml (¼ pint) single cream
300 ml (½ pint) chicken stock
1 tsp Dijon mustard
Salt and freshly ground black pepper
3 tbsp chopped fresh dill

Melt the butter in a saucepan, stir in the flour and cook over a gentle heat for 1-2 minutes, stirring. Heat the cream and the stock together and pour onto the butter mixture. Mix well and simmer for 4 minutes. Stir in the mustard and season. Stir in the dill.

Black Mint

Black mint (Mentha x piperita) is a variety of peppermint, very similar to white peppermint. The main difference is simply one of colour – the leaves and stems of black peppermint are a dark purplish-brown, while those of white peppermint are green.

Black peppermint produces more oil than the white variety, but it is of an inferior quality. The oil is used medicinally to relieve sickness and nausea and its strong flavour and smell mean that it is widely used to disguise the more unpleasant taste of other drugs.

Black mint was grown commercially for its oil as early as 1750. This aromatic variety of mint thrives in a moist, rich soil and a sunny position. It grows to a height of 60-90 cm (2-3 ft) and produces mauve flowers from midsummer.

October

15

16

Plant mint in the garden to keep away ants and beetles.

17

18

19

20

Peppermint tea is usually made from black peppermint. The leaves can either be used on their own or dried and mixed with ordinary tea.

21

Scented Stationery Wallet

A sweetly scented letter is always a pleasure to receive and makes a welcome change from the bills and circular letters that usually arrive through the letter box every day.

You will need:

Large sheet of pretty, hand-made paper
Glue
Ribbon
Dried lavender

1 Cut the hand-made paper into a square measuring 30 x 30 cm (12 x 12 in).

2 Fold two opposite corners into the centre, so that the points are just touching. Fold a third corner in with the point just passing the centre so that it slightly overlaps the edges of the other two flaps. Glue the third flap to the lower two, resulting in a large envelope.

3 Fold down the top flap.

4 Fill the wallet with matching paper and envelopes and add a spoonful of dried lavender to scent the stationery.

5 Tie a length of decorative ribbon around the wallet to keep it closed, and slip of few stems of dried lavender through the bow.

Mint and Lemon Face Mask

This is suitable for an oily skin. Place 1 tsp lemon juice, 1 egg white, half a cucumber (peeled and chopped) and some fresh peppermint leaves in a blender or food processor and purée. Leave the face mask on for 10-15 minutes before rinsing off with tepid water.

> After its first appearance as wedding attire, the best suit was folded away with lavender sprigs in its owner's clothes' chest and only taken out on high days and holidays.
>
> *Still Glides The Stream*
> Flora Thompson

Curry Plant

Curry plant (*Helichrysum italicum*) is a half-hardy perennial evergreen plant, native to the Mediterranean region. It produces slender, silver-grey leaves and clusters of small, yellow flowers which bloom from midsummer. The leaves are aromatic and give off a spicy scent.

This herb prefers a sunny, sheltered position and well drained, sandy soil. It can reach a height of 45 cm (18 in) and is suitable for container growing.

The leaves of the curry plant can be used either fresh or dried to add a curry flavour to soups and stews.

October

22

23

On a warm day the curry plant will scent the air in the garden.

24

25

26

27

'In such a night
Medea gathered the enchanted herbs
That did renew old Aeson.'

The Merchant of Venice
William Shakespeare

28

Knot Gardens

Formal knot gardens date back to the fifteenth century. Gardens are laid out in symmetrical patterns, rather like latticework, with small beds of herbs separated by low, well-manicured box hedges and gravel, paved or bricked pathways. The gardens are often quite secluded places, enclosed within taller hedges or walls.

The herbs are traditionally divided into separate beds of culinary, scented and medicinal herbs. The plants are laid out in intricate patterns and, when looked down on from above, the garden resembles a detailed embroidery or tapestry. The herbs planted in a knot garden should be the shorter varieties and most plants need to be trimmed to the same height several times during the growing season.

A knot garden can be any size, and a miniature version can be planned to fit into the smallest garden. The garden should be planned on paper first. On a scale diagram of the area draw the beds in a symmetrical pattern. Many knot gardens have a central feature, such as a bay tree, sundial or statue, to draw the eye to the centre. Next, decide which herbs you wish to include and position them in the diagrams of the beds, ensuring that you give each bed a similar look in terms of colour and contents. The herbs can either be planted close to each other to provide complete ground cover (and thus avoid weeding) or laid out in a strict geometric pattern.

If you do not wish to plant box hedges, which can be temperamental in some climates and which require a fair amount of attention, plant long 'ribbons' of one or two herbs (such as thyme or marjoram) to separate the different beds.

▲ *A formal herb garden with four symmetrical groups of beds with a central display of terracotta pots.*

▲ *Perfectly drilled herb bushes stand to attention, enclosed by low box hedges, in this geometric knot garden.*

◀ *A knot garden laid out with an elegant central fountain, brick pathways and four herb beds of the same size. One of the beds has been designed as a maze.*

Fennel

Fennel (Foeniculum vulgare) is a hardy perennial with aromatic, feathery leaves which can be either green or bronze in colour. From midsummer it produces bright yellow flowers. Fennel looks very similar to dill, but has a completely different flavour. It grows to a height of 1.5-2 m (5-6 ft) and prefers a well drained soil and plenty of sun.

Fennel is an important culinary herb and its sweet aniseed flavour is a good partner for fish and vegetable dishes. Either the leaves or seeds can be used. Chopped leaves can be scattered over salads or new potatoes and the seeds add flavour to baking.

Fennel is said to be useful in treating eye complaints and strengthening sight; an infusion of fennel leaves and seeds will relieve tired eyes.

'A savoury odour blown,
Grateful to appetite, more pleased my sense
Than smell of sweetest fennel.'

Paradise Lost
John Milton

'Above the lower plants it towers,
The fennel with its yellow flowers;
And in an earlier age than ours
Was gifted with the wondrous powers
Lost vision to restore.'

Henry Wadsworth Longfellow

October

29

In medieval times fennel was hung on doors on Midsummer's Eve to ward off evil spirits.

30

31

Fennel is said to provide strength and courage and promote longevity.

Sautéed Lamb with Fennel and Orange

Serves 4

Serve this lamb dish with rice and a garnish of orange slices as a dinner party main course.

60 g (2 tbsp) butter or margarine
675 g (1½ lb) neck fillets of lamb
3 shallots, finely chopped
30 g (2 tbsp) flour
340 ml (¾ pint) stock
Grated rind and juice of 1 orange
30 g (2 tbsp) chopped fennel tops
1 bay leaf
Salt and freshly ground black pepper
1 orange, peeled and sliced, as garnish

1 Melt the butter or margarine in a frying pan. Cut the lamb into 1.25 cm (½ in) slices and quickly brown on both sides. Remove and keep warm.

2 Lower the heat and cook the shallots to soften them. Remove from the pan.

3 Add the flour to the pan and brown slowly, stirring frequently to prevent sticking and burning. When golden brown, pour in the stock, orange juice and rind and bring to the boil to mix thoroughly.

4 Return the lamb and shallots to the pan and add the fennel, bay leaf and seasoning. Cover the pan and simmer for 40 minutes or until tender. Remove the bay leaf before serving.

Herb Vinegars

White wine vinegars flavoured with herbs can be used in all types of recipes, including salad dressings, mayonnaise and sauces. They are an excellent way of adding the flavour of herbs, especially during winter when fresh herbs may not be available. Experiment with different herbs until you find a particular vinegar you enjoy.

The following herbs all make good vinegars:

Basil vinegar – pound the basil leaves in warm vinegar to release their flavour, strain the vinegar and bottle.
Bay leaf vinegar – add the leaves to warmed vinegar.
Dill vinegar – place fresh dill leaves in vinegar. Dill seeds can also be added.
Elderflower vinegar – add elderflowers to vinegar.
Lavender vinegar – add lavender flowers, rather than stalks.
Rosemary vinegar – add several sprigs of rosemary.
Tarragon vinegar – add fresh tarragon leaves.

A mixed herb vinegar can be made with your own selection of herbs.

A spicy vinegar can be made by adding cloves of garlic, black or red peppercorns, chilli peppers and celery seed.

Rinse for Chapped Hands

Make an infusion of 600 ml (1 pint) boiling water and 2 tbsp of either marigold petals, fennel, comfrey or chamomile flowers. Cool and strain the liquid. After washing your hands, rinse them in the cold infusion.

Fennel Tea

Fennel tea can be made from either the leaves or the seeds of this herb. If using seeds, bruise them first to help release the flavour. Sweeten the tea with a spoonful of honey. The tea is a mild laxative.

Yogurt and Fennel Cleanser

Make a fennel infusion of 2 tbsp fennel leaves to 150 ml (5 fl oz) boiling water and leave to cool. Mix 150 g (5 oz) natural yogurt with the cold infusion and pour into clean bottles.

November

Elder

Elder (Sambucas nigra) is a hardy deciduous shrub or tree. There are two varieties – the European elder grows to a height of 7 m (22 ft), while the smaller, shrubbier American variety reaches a height of 3 m (12 ft). Its creamy white flowers bloom in early summer and produce a beautiful scent, while its berries ripen by the end of summer and are often eaten by birds. The elder can be found growing wild in many hedgerows, so flowers and berries can often be gathered on country walks.

The elder has many medicinal and culinary uses. Elderflowers can be made into wine with a flavour similar to that of the muscatel grape or a delicious champagne. The flowers can also be added to fruit dishes, made into cordials or sorbets and ice creams. The berries can also be made into wine or be used in jam-making.

Medicinally, elder has been used to treat many illnesses, including inflammations of the mouth, epilepsy and croup.

November

1

2

'An elder stake and a blackthorn ether (hedge)
Will make a hedge to last for ever'

3

4

5

Cheap port can be made to resemble the superior tawny port by the addition of elderberry juice.

6

7

Pot Pourri Presents

Pretty boxes of pot pourri make lovely presents which the lucky recipient can enjoy for many months.

The gifts are even more appreciated if the pot pourri is home-made. During the summer, gather a good variety of herb flowers and leaves for drying. Keep the dried herbs in separate containers and mix special combinations of herbs to suit the person the gift is for.

Hoard pretty boxes whenever you come across them – luxury chocolates are often packed in boxes far too attractive to throw away – or look in stationers and craft shops where you can often find a good selection. Choose boxes in colours to coordinate with the pot pourri. Here the small circular box in shades of blue and violet contains lavender, while the oval pink and green box holds an aromatic blend of rose petals and assorted mint leaves.

Close the boxes with matching ribbons and gift tags.

Elderflower Champagne

Makes approximately 7 x 75 cl bottles

Despite its name, elderflower 'champagne' is a non-alcoholic drink. It is simply called champagne because of the bubbles! Store this fizzy, country drink for 2-3 weeks before opening.

8 heads of elderflowers
4.5 litres (8 pints) boiling water
550 g (1¼ lb) sugar
30 ml (2 tbsp) white wine vinegar
2 lemons, sliced

1 Place the elderflowers, sugar, vinegar and lemons in a very large bowl or wine-making drum and pour over the boiling water.

2 Stir the mixture to dissolve the sugar. Cover the bowl or drum and stand in a warm place for 24 hours.

3 Strain the liquid into a jug (you will need to do this gradually) and pour into clean wine bottles. Seal the bottles with corks and store in a cool, dark place for 2-3 weeks.

Honey and Elderflower Cleanser

This cleanser will suit all skin types. Place 16 tbsp natural yogurt and 5 tbsp elderflowers in a saucepan and heat very gently over a low heat for 30 minutes. Remove from the heat and leave to infuse for 4-5 hours. Melt 2½ tbsp clear honey. Reheat the yogurt mixture and strain out the elderflowers. Add the melted honey and mix well. Pour into clean bottles and store in the refrigerator.

Golden Feverfew

Golden feverfew (Chrysanthemum parthenium) is very similar to the more common feverfew, except that its flowers are a much brighter, richer yellow. It is a fairly fast growing, bushy perennial with aromatic green leaves and flowers which last from early summer through to autumn. In well drained soil and full sun it can reach a height of 60 cm (2 ft).

It has been used to treat nervousness, hysteria and low spirits, and a decoction mixed with honey or sugar relieves coughs and breathing difficulties. Fresh feverfew leaves are still used today to treat migraine. However, feverfew should not be used if you are pregnant as its stimulant effect on the womb may induce labour.

November

8

9

Feverfew's name comes from the word 'febrifuge', meaning 'indicating fever', for its tonic and fever-dispelling powers.

10

11

12

13

14

Feverfew tincture will sooth insect and vermin bites.

Propagating Herbs

Rather than buying plants from garden centres or herb farms, many people grow herb gardens simply from cuttings begged from friends and neighbours. The nice thing about this is that the plants will then always remind you of that particular person.

Herbs can be propagated in three different ways:

Layering

This is the easiest way to produce new plants, but can only be done with herbs growing in beds rather than pots. This method works well with the woodier herbs, such as mint, marjoram, southernwood, rosemary, sage and lemon balm. Select a strong branch growing close to the ground. On the underside of the stem, make a slanting, upward cut halfway through it. Put some hormone rooting powder on the slit. Bend the branch down and bury the cut in the soil so that just the leaves at the end of the stem are visible above the soil. Anchor the branch in the soil with a V-shaped piece of garden wire. After several weeks the cut will have produced roots and the new plant can be gently dug up.

Dividing roots

This should be done when the herbs are lying dormant and there is no danger of frost. Carefully dig up the plant and divide the clump of roots into several smaller plants.

Stem cuttings

Take healthy cuttings of about 10 cm (4 in) in length from the main plants. Strip the lower leaves from the stem and dip in water and then rooting powder. Plant the cuttings in moist cutting compost or sand. The cuttings will take root within several weeks.

Hop

The hop (Humulus lupulus) is a perennial vine which, in the wild, grows over bushes, hedges and trees. If cultivated in a garden, it makes a good screen if it has proper support, such as a fence or trellis. Hops need plenty of sun and a rich soil to thrive.

The hop produces yellowish-green female 'cones' which contain flowers and embryonic fruits. When dried, these are the parts of the plant that have been used to flavour beer since the Middle Ages. The young shoots and immature leaves can be added to vegetable soups or cooked on their own and tossed in butter.

Hops have a slight sedative effect and are used to treat insomnia. An infusion of dried hops drunk at bedtime will encourage a good night's sleep. The dried flowers can be added to ordinary tea to stimulate the appetite.

November

15

16

Hop juice was once drunk to cleanse the blood.

17

18

Hop leaves and flowers can be used to produce a natural brown dye.

19

20

21

Spicy Spanish Chicken

Serves 6

Coriander mixed with spices adds a warm Spanish flavour to grilled chicken. Wear rubber gloves when preparing the chilli pepper to avoid skin irritation.

6 boned chicken breasts
Grated rind and juice of 1 lime
30 ml (2 tbsp) olive oil
Coarsely ground black pepper
90 ml (6 tbsp) whole grain mustard
10 ml (2 tsp) paprika
4 ripe tomatoes
2 shallots, chopped
1 clove garlic, crushed
½ chilli pepper, seeded and chopped
5 ml (1 tsp) wine vinegar
Pinch of salt
30 ml (2 tbsp) chopped fresh coriander
Whole coriander leaves, to garnish

1 Place the chicken breasts in a shallow dish with the lime rind and juice, oil, mustard, pepper and paprika. Marinate for 1 hour, turning occasionally.

2 Peel the tomatoes by dropping them into boiling water for about 5 seconds or less depending on ripeness. Place immediately in cold water and the peel should come off easily. Quarter and seed the tomatoes.

3 Place the tomatoes, shallots, garlic, chilli pepper, vinegar and salt in a food processor or blender and process until coarsely chopped. Stir in the coriander.

4 Place the chicken skin side up on a grill pan, reserving the marinade. Cook the chicken for 7-10 minutes, depending on how close the chicken is to the heat source. Baste frequently with the marinade. Turn the chicken and grill the other side in the same way. Sprinkle with salt after grilling.

5 Place the chicken on serving plates. Garnish with coriander and serve a spoonful of tomato relish on one side.

Buttered Hops

Soak a handful of young hop shoots in a bowl of cold water with several spoonfuls of salt. Drain and place in a saucepan of just enough boiling water to cover the hops. Boil until the shoots are tender. Drain the shoots, add salt and pepper and a knob of butter to the pan and chop up the hops.

Keep a jug of freshly picked herbs in the kitchen so you have fresh herbs immediately at hand when cooking, making herbal teas or remedies. Included here are lemon balm, purple sage, variegated mint, feverfew, lavender and marigolds.

Henry VII ruled that hops should not be added to beer as they were believed to be 'wicked weeds that would spoil the taste of the drink and endanger the people'.

Fragrant Fires

Don't discard the dried stems of herbs once the leaves or flowerheads have been picked off for pot pourri. Group together the dried stems of herbs such as rosemary, lavender, lemon verbena and thyme and tie into bundles with string. When added to open fires, the heat releases the fragrance of the herbs and scents the room.

Winter Savory

Winter savory (*Satureia montana*) is a hardy evergreen perennial native to southern Europe which thrives in well drained soil and plenty of sun. It differs from summer savory in that it has larger leaves and does not have such spreading growth. Growing to a height of 30 cm (1 ft), winter savory has slender, dull green leaves and pale mauve flowers which bloom in late summer.

Tall winter savory plants should be cut back to their woody base each spring to encourage new growth.

This herb has a peppery taste and is used in meat dishes. It can also be added to herb mixtures to provide a hotter, spicier flavour. Finely chopped leaves can be added to butter.

Winter savory is not widely used medicinally, but is well worth growing as a garden plant.

November

22

Winter savory is an insect repellant so it is a good herb
to plant near the house.

23

24

25

26

'Here's flowers for you;
Hot lavender, mints, savory, marjoram.'

The Winter's Tale
William Shakespeare

27

28

Herbal Bath Oils

Bath oils give a luxurious, relaxing feeling to bathtime and also soften hard water, which can leave the skin feeling dry. Collect old perfume bottles or glass jars with glass stoppers to display the oils in your bathroom.

There are two different ways to make herbal bath oils.

1 Buy a bottle of almond or apricot kernel oil and decant into smaller bottles. Add a couple of drops of a herb essential oil, such as lavender, mint, thyme or rosemary and shake the bottle gently to mix the oils thoroughly. Add a few drops of the scented oil to running bath water.

2 Add sprigs of flowering herbs such as lavender or rosemary to bottles of almond or apricot kernel oil and leave in a warm place for several weeks for the oil to absorb the herbs' scent. Stir or shake the mixture daily. Strain the oil and add a couple of spoonfuls to the bath water.

Swiss Cheese Layer

Serves 4

Serve these ramekins of savoury cheese as a starter.

120 g (4 oz) Emmenthal cheese, grated
15 ml (1 tbsp) chopped fresh borage leaves
4 eggs
Salt and freshly ground black pepper
120 g (4 oz) Gruyère cheese, grated
10 ml (2 tsp) chopped fresh savory
30 g (1 oz) cornchips, crushed

1 Mix the Emmenthal cheese and borage together and divide between 4 ramekins.

2 Crack an egg into each dish and season to taste.

3 Mix the Gruyère cheese with the savory and spoon on top of the egg. Sprinkle the top with crushed corn chips.

4 Arrange the ramekins in the microwave in a circle and cook on LOW for 3-5 minutes until the cheese melts and the eggs are cooked.

Vervain

Vervain (Verbena officinalis) is a perennial herb with sparsely-leafed upright stems and pale lilac flowers. It grows to a height of 45 cm (18 in) and prefers to grow in a sheltered position. It is often found growing wild on roadsides, wasteground and in hedgerows.

Vervain is an unscented herb with a slightly bitter taste. It has a variety of medicinal uses, including being used to treat pleurisy and ulcers, various illnesses linked to the stomach, liver and kidneys, in a poultice to relieve headaches and rheumatic pains, and as a general tonic.

Vervain was believed to possess magical and aphrodisiac properties and was once widely used in various rites and incantations associated with witchcraft and sorcery.

November

29

According to legend, vervain was used on the Mount of Calvary to staunch Christ's wounds.

30

Roman soldiers carried vervain to protect them in battle.

Begin your Christmas preparations early and make these attractive lavender-filled doves to decorate your Christmas tree, or as scented gifts to delight your family and friends.

Christmas Dove

This small, lavender-filled dove can be used to decorate a Christmas tree and the warmth of the room will release its sweet scent. Use either fabrics in the traditional red and green colours of Christmas or, for a more elegant look, choose white, gold or silver fabrics.

You will need:

Small scraps of fabric
Two 25 cm (9 in) lengths of ribbon
Terylene wadding
Two sequins
Two small bells
Dried lavender

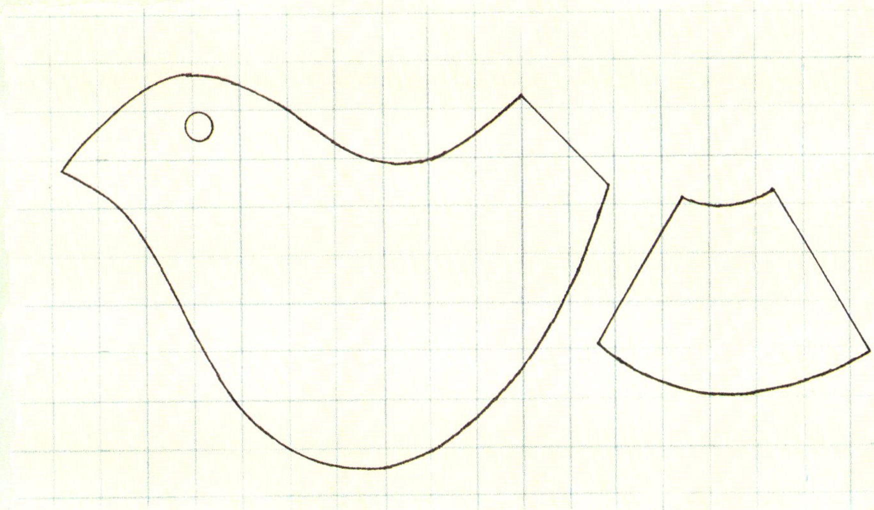

Each square represents 1cm
Body – cut 2
(Remember to reverse pattern piece)
Tail – cut 2
Add ½cm seam allowance.

1 Trace off the templates. Cut out one piece of fabric for the body. Reverse the body template and cut another piece of fabric. Cut out two pieces of fabric for the tail.

2 Pin the body pieces together, right sides facing. Pin the hanging length of ribbon into the seam at the top edge of the body, so that the ends are sewn in. Pin the length of ribbon for the bell into the underside of the body, so that the two ends will be left dangling.

3 Carefully sew the two body pieces together, leaving an opening at the tail end. Make sure the ribbons do not get caught up in the seams, except at the correct positions. Turn right sides out – you may need to snip the seam edges slightly to avoid bulky seams. Stuff the body with wadding and dried lavender.

4 To make the tail, pin fabric pieces right sides together and sew around three sides. Turn right sides out, stuff with wadding and hem the fourth side.

5 Sew the tail to the body. Stitch on two sequins for eyes and attach bells to the lower ribbon.

Strewing Herbs

During Medieval times strewing herbs became popular, although the practice actually dates back to ancient Roman times. These were mixtures of herbs literally scattered over the floors of houses with the dual purpose of sweetening the air of musty rooms and disguising the smells due to poor hygiene, lack of running water and, very often, the close proximity of farm animals. Herbs such as sage, meadowsweet, costmary, basil, lavender, hyssop and rose petals were used.

History reports that strewing herbs were used to such an extent at one Roman banquet that several guests actually suffocated as a result of the huge quantity of rose petals showered upon them by servants.

December

Opal Basil

Opal basil (Ocimum basilicum 'Purpurascens'), also known as purple-leaf basil, is a variety of the more usual green basil. This variety has dark, purply-red leaves, stems and flowers and is often grown as a decorative garden plant. Like other varieties of basil, opal basil thrives in warm, sunny climates and can be damaged by frost. It needs a rich, damp soil and a sheltered position.

Opal basil has the same distinctive clove-like smell as green basil and grows into a small, bushy plant ideal for container growing. Encourage the plant to grow into a bushy shape by pinching out the growing tips.

The oil of basil is extracted on a commercial basis and used in the perfumery industry.

The Herb of Love

In parts of Italy basil is considered a token of love. Young single girls place a pot of basil on their windowsill or doorstep to indicate they are not 'spoken for' and would welcome the attention of suitors.

December

1

In India basil is sacred to the gods Vishnu and Krishna and is cherished in Hindu homes.

2

3

4

Travel sickness can be prevented by drinking a cold infusion of basil leaves before beginning a journey.

5

6

7

Scorpions and Basil

Old superstitions linked basil with scorpions and it was believed that if a sprig of basil was left under a flowerpot, it would turn into a scorpion. Using the theory of like attracts like, it was thought that if a basil leaf was applied to a poisonous bite or a bee or wasp sting, it would draw the poison to it. Basil seeds were also thought to be an antidote to snake poison and were taken internally and laid on the bite.

Herbed Vegetable Strips

Serves 4

Serve these vegetable ribbons as a side dish with grilled meat, poultry or fish. Parmesan cheese may be sprinkled on top for extra flavour.

2 large courgettes, ends trimmed
2 medium carrots, peeled
1 large or 2 small leeks, trimmed, halved and well washed
120 g (4 oz) walnuts
1 small onion, chopped
30 g (2 tbsp) chopped parsley
15 g (1 tbsp) dried basil
280-400 ml (½-¾ pint) olive oil
Salt and freshly ground black pepper

1 Cut the courgettes and carrots into long, thin strips. Cut the leeks into lengths the same size, making sure they are well rinsed between all the layers, and cut into thin strips.

2 Place the carrot strips in a pan of boiling water and cook for about 3-4 minutes or until tender crisp. Drain and rinse under cold water.

3 Cook the courgette strips separately for about 2-3 minutes and add the leek strips during the last minute of cooking. Drain and rinse the vegetables and leave with the carrots to drain dry.

4 Place the walnuts, onions, parsley and basil in the bowl of a food processor or in a blender and chop finely.

5 Reserve about 45 ml (3 tbsp) of the olive oil for later use. With the machine running, pour the remaining olive oil through the funnel in a thin, steady stream. Use enough oil to bring the mixture to the consistency of mayonnaise. Add seasoning to taste.

6 Place the reserved oil in a large pan and heat. When hot, add the drained vegetables. Season and toss over a moderate heat until heated through. Add the herb and walnut sauce and toss gently to coat the vegetables. Serve immediately.

Rock Hyssop

Rock hyssop (Hyssop officinalis) is very similar to hyssop but slightly bushier in appearance. It should not be confused with hedge hyssop which is poisonous. Native to southern Europe, rock hyssop produces pink, blue and mauve flowers in summer and is a good edging plant to grow.

Hyssop leaves or dried hyssop flowers can be used to make a medicinal tea which is sweetened with honey. It was once prescribed to be taken by the wineglassful three times daily 'for debility of the chest'.

Hyssop is a strongly flavoured herb and was one of the strewing herbs because of its fragrance. The green tops of the plant can be boiled in soup to help treat asthma.

December

8

9

10

11

Radishes will not grow well if planted too close to hyssop.

12

13

14

Mixed Vegetable and Prawn Risotto

Serves 4

This quick-to-prepare recipe flavoured with pennyroyal and hyssop makes an ideal supper dish.

15 ml (1 tbsp) oil
½ red pepper, seeded and diced
½ green pepper, seeded and diced
570 ml (1 pint) hot vegetable stock
225 g (8 oz) brown rice
180 g (6 oz) button mushrooms, quartered
2 tsp chopped fresh pennyroyal
2 tsp chopped fresh hyssop
Salt and freshly ground black pepper
120 g (4 oz) prawns

1 Put the oil in a casserole and add the diced peppers. Cover and cook on HIGH for 3-4 minutes until the peppers begin to soften.

2 Add the stock, rice, mushroom, herbs and seasoning. Stir, cover and cook on HIGH for 25-30 minutes or until most of the liquid has been absorbed.

3 Stir in the prawns and leave to stand for 5 minutes before serving.

Raspberry Cordial

This is a rich pink, concentrated cordial flavoured with hyssop. For a refreshing drink, dilute with fizzy mineral water and served in glasses filled with ice cubes.

Place 1 kg (2¼ lb) of raspberries in a large saucepan and heat very gently, stirring, until the raspberry juice is released and they almost come up to a boil. Place a nylon sieve over a large bowl and pour the fruit into the sieve. Press the fruit gently with a spoon to extract as much juice as possible. Put the raspberry juice into a saucepan with 340 g (12 oz) granulated sugar, a couple of sprigs of fresh hyssop and the juice of one lemon. Heat gently until the sugar has dissolved, stirring all the time to make sure the sugar does not catch on the bottom of the pan. Strain the cordial to remove the herbs, allow to cool and then bottle.

Bay

Bay (Laurus nobilis) is an evergreen tree with glossy green leaves, olive green or red bark, and small, creamy-white flowers which bloom from midsummer. A native of the Mediterranean region, it is also known as laurel and sweet bay. This is the only type of laurel which can be used in cooking. Although slow-growing, it can grow up to 8 m (26 ft) in height and prefers a sheltered, sunny position and rich, well drained soil.

Bay trees are ideal to grow in containers which means they can be brought indoors during severe winter weather.

Bay leaves are one of the three herbs used in a classic bouquet garni. They can be added to marinades, the poaching water for fish, soups and stews. Use the leaves whole as the oil contained within the leaf is extremely strong and always remember to remove them before serving.

December

15

16

Bay leaves can be slowly dried in the shade and then stored in tightly sealed jars.

17

18

Bay leaves were woven into the laurel wreaths used to crown victors and heroes in ancient Rome.

19

20

'Say, Britain, could you ever boast,
Three poets in an age at most?
Our chilling climate hardly bears
A sprig of bays in fifty years.'

Jonathan Swift

21

Mussels à la Greque

Serves 4

Make this dish when mussels are at their best, usually in autumn and winter. The shells of fresh mussels must be tightly closed and intact. Any that are cracked or do not shut tight when tapped with a knife should be discarded. Any mussels that stay shut after being cooked should also be thrown away.

1.2 litres (2 pints) mussels
1 onion, chopped
120 ml (4 fl oz) white wine
Lemon juice
2 tbsp olive oil
1 clove garlic, peeled and crushed
1 shallot or 2 spring onions, chopped
675 g (1½ lb) fresh tomatoes, chopped
1 tsp fennel seeds
1 tsp coriander seeds
1 tsp crushed oregano
1 bay leaf
1 tbsp chopped fresh basil
Pinch of cayenne pepper
Salt and freshly ground black pepper
Black olives, to garnish

1 Scrub the mussels and discard any with broken shells or which do not shut when tapped with a knife.

2 Put the mussels in a large saucepan with the onion, wine and lemon juice. Cover and cook quickly until the mussels open, discarding any that do not.

3 Remove the mussels from their shells and leave to cool. Reserve the cooking liquid.

4 Heat the olive oil in a saucepan and add the garlic and the shallot or spring onions. Cook gently until golden brown.

5 Stir in the tomatoes, spices and herbs. Season to taste and blend in the reserved liquor from the mussels. Bring the mixture to the boil and allow to boil rapidly until the tomatoes are soft and the liquid is reduced by half. Remove the bay leaf.

6 Allow the sauce to cool, then stir in the mussels. Chill well and serve garnished with black olives and with a green salad and French bread.

Bay trees are ideal to grow in pots. Prune them regularly to achieve a slender, leafless trunk and a round ball of leaves at the top. Bay trees look good in the centre of knot or formal herb gardens, or standing to attention either side of elegant doorways.

The title of Poet Laureate takes its name from the bay or laurel tree. In ancient Rome eminent poets were awarded laurel wreaths.

Garden Sage

Garden sage (*Salvia officinalis*) is the most common of the many varieties of green sage. It is a strongly flavoured, aromatic evergreen shrub which can grow to a height of 120 cm (4 ft). This variety produces purple flowers and soft green leaves which have a rough texture.

Sage will grow in almost any well drained soil in a sunny position. Other green varieties include golden sage, which has gold-tipped leaves, pineapple sage, variegated-leaf sage, which has green leaves flecked with cream, and tricolour sage, which produces grey-green leaves speckled with white, purple and pink.

Sage is widely used in Italian cooking and is one of the herbs often used in stuffings for poultry. In Italy sage was believed to preserve health and country folk would eat bread and butter sandwiches filled with sage leaves.

December

22

Sage tea was believed to cleanse and purify the blood.

23

24

25

26

27

In Jamaica sage tea is served sweetened with lime juice.

28

Herb Stuffing for Poultry

Fresh herbs are ideal to use in stuffings. Ring the changes by using a variety of different herbs such as thyme, parsley, rosemary or sage.

Sage and Onion Stuffing

50 g (2 oz) butter
1 onion, peeled and chopped
75 g (3 oz) breadcrumbs
3 tbsp chopped sage
Salt and freshly ground black pepper
1 egg, beaten
4 tbsp milk

Melt the butter in a frying pan and cook the onion until slightly coloured. Remove from the heat and stir in the breadcrumbs, sage, salt and pepper. Stir the beaten egg into the mixture and add the milk. Mix thoroughly. This stuffing goes well with pork or duck.

Parsley Stuffing

50 g (2 oz) cooked rice
1 small onion, peeled and chopped
50 g (2 oz) raisins
50 g (2 oz) almonds, blanched and chopped
2 tbsp chopped parsley
30 g (1 oz) butter, melted
1 egg, beaten

Place all the ingredients in a large bowl, season and mix together thoroughly. Use this stuffing with chicken, fish or meat.

Christmas Gifts

Prepare last-minute Christmas gifts for unexpected guests. Mix up instant pot pourris from the flowers and leaves you have dried throughout the year and pack them into pretty boxes. Scented bath oils and bath sachets will make welcome gifts, and bottles of elderflower champagne can be opened to toast the occasion.

Salad Burnet

Salad Burnet (Poterium sanguisorba) is a hardy perennial which grows to about 30 cm (12 in) in height. It has pale green, jagged-edged leaves and small red flowers which bloom for the whole summer. Originally from the Mediterranean region, it will grow in poor soil and either sun or light shade.

The leaves should be harvested regularly and the flowers cut off to encourage new growth. The leaves have a taste similar to cucumber and can be added to salads, raw vegetable dishes or fruit cups and punches.

A decoction of salad burnet leaves mixed with honey was once used to treat various complaints, including gout and rheumatism, and an infusion of the leaves worked well as an astringent.

December

29

Salad burnet was introduced to America by the Pilgrim Fathers.

30

Salad burnet leaves were once used to flavour claret and other drinks.

31

Pasta with Fresh Tomato and Basil Sauce

Serves 6

Pasta is the perfect ingredient to cook in large quantities if you have a house full of hungry guests on New Year's Eve. It is quick to cook, which means you won't have to spend the whole evening in the kitchen and the sauce can be made in advance and frozen. Simply double the quantities if you are feeding a large party. Serve with plenty of good red wine!

1 small onion, finely chopped
450 g (1 lb) fresh tomatoes
30 ml (2 tbsp) tomato purée
Grated rind and juice of 1 orange
2 cloves garlic, peeled and crushed
Salt and freshly ground black pepper
140 ml (¼ pint) red wine
140 ml (¼ pint) chicken stock
30 ml (2 tbsp) coarsely chopped basil
340 g (12 oz) wholemeal pasta

1 Cut a small cross in the skins of the tomatoes and plunge them into boiling water for 30 seconds. Remove the blanched tomatoes from the water and carefully peel away the loosened skin.

2 Cut the tomatoes in quarters, and remove and discard the pips. Chop the tomato flesh roughly and put in a large saucepan with the onion and tomato purée.

3 Heat the onion and tomatoes over a low heat, stirring continuously until the tomatoes soften and begin to lose their juice.

4 Add the orange rind and juice to the saucepan with all the remaining ingredients, apart from the pasta, and bring to the boil. Continue to boil until the sauce has reduced and the vegetables are soft.

5 While the sauce is cooking, put the pasta into another saucepan with enough boiling water to cover. Season with salt and cook for 10-15 minutes or until the pasta is soft.

6 Drain the pasta and stir it into the hot tomato sauce. Serve immediately.

Decorate the house for New Year's Eve festivities with wreaths and swags of green foliage and herbs. Buy undecorated straw or raffia wreaths and swags from florists or craft shops, and florists' wire to attach the herbs. First, attach a background of green foliage such as holly, bay, rosemary or whatever is available from your garden. Add small scented bunches of fragrant herbs such as dried lavender or dried roses. As the house warms up, their fragrance will be released. Fill any gaps with small ribbon bows.

Salad Burnet Vinegar

Half fill a wide-necked glass storage jar with fresh burnet leaves and pour in enough red wine vinegar to fill the jar. Leave for several weeks before straining the vinegar and using in recipes.

Index

Dates refer to the first date on each spread.